THE UNITED STATES
AS A NEIGHBOUR

T0381586

LECTURES DELIVERED ON THE
SIR GEORGE WATSON FOUNDATION
FOR AMERICAN HISTORY, LITERATURE,
AND INSTITUTIONS

THE UNITED STATES AS A NEIGHBOUR

from a Canadian Point of View

BY

SIR ROBERT FALCONER

K·C·M·G

PRESIDENT OF THE
UNIVERSITY OF
TORONTO

CAMBRIDGE

AT THE UNIVERSITY PRESS

1925

CAMBRIDGE
UNIVERSITY PRESS

University Printing House, Cambridge CB2 8BS, United Kingdom

Published in the United States of America by Cambridge University Press, New York

Cambridge University Press is part of the University of Cambridge.

It furthers the University's mission by disseminating knowledge in the pursuit of education, learning and research at the highest international levels of excellence.

www.cambridge.org
Information on this title: www.cambridge.org/9781107657656

© Cambridge University Press 1925

First published 1925
First paperback edition 2014

A catalogue record for this publication is available from the British Library

ISBN 978-1-107-65765-6 Paperback

PREFACE

THE purpose of the Sir George Watson Chair of American History and Institutions is to promote good relations between the two great branches of the English-speaking world by the annual delivery of lectures on American History in British Universities. It was decided by the Trustees of the Foundation that this purpose would be served this year if the course were given by a Canadian, who might present aspects of the history of the United States as they appear to her northern neighbour. I am very grateful to the Trustees for having chosen me for this honour.

The opening lecture was given in the Mansion House, London, the Lord Mayor presiding, and it was followed by single lectures in the Universities of Oxford, Cambridge, Manchester, Edinburgh, Glasgow and Belfast, delivered in the months of May and June, 1925. For the kindly welcome extended to me everywhere I wish to take this opportunity of expressing my warm thanks.

In the preparation of the lectures I have received valuable aid from many friends, but I must refer especially to James White, Esq., of the Department of Justice, Ottawa, Dr A. H. U. Colquhoun, Deputy

Minister of Education, Ontario, Principal E. H. Oliver, Saskatoon, Dean Pakenham, W. S. Wallace, Esq. and Professor Innis; the last three of the University of Toronto.

To H. S. Perris, Esq., M.A., Director of the Anglo-American Society, I am deeply indebted for unfailing courtesy and helpfulness.

R·A·FALCONER

September 3, 1925

CONTENTS

Chapter V

TRADE AND COMMERCE

Chapter VI

THE WORLD OF THE AVERAGE MAN

Chapter VII

THE WORLD OF HIGHER EDUCATION

Chapter VIII

CANADA AS INTERPRETER

★

MAP OF CANADA, showing boundaries

available for download from www.cambridge.org/9781107657656

CHAPTER I

Common Elements of Population

AMERICANS of Anglo-Saxon origin and English-speaking Canadians are more alike than any other separate peoples. Not even among the associated nations of the British Commonwealth does there exist such a substantial community of ideals and manners. The estranging ocean has kept Australia and New Zealand from intimacy with Canada, and of South Africa even less is known in the northern Dominion. But the older American is a genuine neighbour to the Canadian. Without much effort each finds himself reasonably comfortable in the home of the other, though each has managed his own household in the way he deemed of most advantage to himself.

The term "American" is given to citizens of the United States on the assumption that there is a common national life within the borders of this vast Republic, that the people of all the states that constitute it respond to similar political and social ideals, and that they are devoted to the flag which is an emblem of their principles and their common security. In Canada or in Europe the American is known at once, whether he comes from Maine or from California, from Wisconsin or from Georgia. So also the term "Canadian" is employed as expressive of a unified national sentiment among the provinces of the Dominion. That such a sentiment exists is obvious to any one who has lived long enough in the different provinces to understand the life of their several communities. Halifax is more like Victoria than the former is like Portland, Maine, or the latter like Portland, Oregon. Toronto resembles Winnipeg more than the former resembles Buffalo or the latter Minneapolis. And in spite of difference of language and social and religious institutions the province of Quebec is closer in spirit to the Maritime provinces or to Ontario than to any of the United States.

But within these two comprehensive national units there are well-defined groups or regions, with characteristics and interests of their own. Professor Turner[1] has recently stated that the Americans are in reality a federation of sections rather than of states, and that these sections fall geographically into such groups as New England, the middle-eastern Atlantic states, the north-central, the north-western, the south-eastern, the south-western and those on the Pacific coast, each pursuing a path of its own in industry, politics and culture. Within Canada

[1] Prof. F. J. Turner, "Sections and Nation," *Yale Review*, Oct. 1922.

also section is so definitely separated from section by natural barriers that groups are taking shape. The Maritime provinces lie far from the thickly settled parts of Quebec and Ontario; these again are cut off by a northern wilderness, hitherto but thinly occupied, from the provinces on the prairie, and British Columbia is withdrawn behind her mountains. Indeed, nothing but a powerful common purpose could have enabled Canadians to triumph over geography as they have done.

In considering the relationship between the United States and Canada it is necessary to restrict our view to the definite areas along the border where the people come into contact with one another. In a night the crossing is made from Nova Scotia to Boston; for many years a decision was in the balance which, if adverse, would have allowed New Brunswick no access to Quebec by the St John River except through the state of Maine; Quebec province lies athwart New England; Ontario looks at her neighbour on the further banks of navigable rivers or great lakes thronged by traffic; on the prairies an astronomical boundary separates the two countries; and the Rockies, the Selkirks and the Coast Range with their intervening valleys run north and south. In view of this easy passage and the similar geographical conditions, the reciprocal influences are chiefly felt in the northern states from the Atlantic to the

Pacific, reaching on that coast as far south as California. In many respects the people of these sections resemble Canadians in character more than their own nationals in the South-East or the South-West.

Furthermore, for our purpose a separation must be made between the Americans of Anglo-Saxon origin who have been in the country for some generations, and the more recent arrivals from central, south or south-eastern Europe. Among the former are to be found, according to the Americans themselves, the genuine and dominating ideals of the nation, which were asserted, for example, after much searching of heart, when it entered the Great War in April, 1917. In so far as the two countries are in sympathy it is in respect of the similarity between this portion of the American people and the English-speaking Canadians. It is necessary, therefore, to estimate the proportion of the older Americans to the whole population of the country. Fortunately, a record of the first census taken in the United States, that of 1790, is available. The loyalists had then left or had been absorbed. The people were predominantly agriculturalist and poor, but cities were rising; Philadelphia with a population of 42,000, New York with 33,000 and Boston with 18,000. Of the total population of 3,930,000, there were 3,172,000 white and 757,000 coloured, and as shown by the names recorded almost the whole white population, except in sections of New York, Pennsylvania and North Carolina, was of English or Scottish origin. Immigration on a large scale began about 1810, and at the end of 1850 2,700,000 people had come in, but still nearly 86 per cent. of all the foreign-born were natives of either the British Isles or Germany. During the sixty years between 1790 and 1850, the most determining factor in the life of the country was the occupation of the West. Much of the best blood of the eastern states, together with immigrants from Britain and North Europe, was poured into Ohio, Indiana, Illinois, Iowa, Kansas, and to this day the people of these states retain many of the essential qualities of the oldest stratum of the nation. Thereafter during the four years of the Civil War this stock suffered severely, the flower of their youth being cut off.

When the census of 1890 was taken, General Walker observed that the enormous immigration of the preceding forty years had introduced a fundamental change into the character of the people; "It amounted not to a reinforcement of the population but to a replacement of native by foreign stock." During the first twenty years of this century 10,700,000 of the 16,000,000 who entered the country came from Russia, Italy, Austria-Hungary, Poland and the Balkans. Unlike those from northern Europe and Britain, they settled in blocks in the industrial centres and have swollen the cities with elements hard to assimilate.

In view of this immigration it is difficult to estimate exactly what proportion of the present population is descended from the original American stock, but "at the twelfth census (1890) the total white population of the continental United States appears to have been divided between descendants of persons enumerated at the second census and of persons who became inhabitants of the United States in the proportion of 35 to 32." As we have seen, the immigration up to 1850 had probably a sufficiently large British infusion to give a long lead to those who maintained Anglo-Saxon ideals and civilization. In 1920 native whites of original stock probably numbered over 47,000,000 or about 50 per cent. of the total white population. Estimating from the last two census reports the proportion of British and Canadian born of British origin living in the United States to the whole number of foreign-born whites at one-sixth, it is not hazardous to conjecture that at present over 56 per cent. of the white American people inherit and promote the Anglo-Saxon tradition[1].

This being, then, the proportion of their neighbours with whom English-speaking Canadians may regard themselves as having affinity, we may con-

[1] W. S. Rossiter, *Increase of Population in the United States, 1910–20*, chapters IX and X, and Appendix A.

sider the movements of population that have affected them both and severally. While it is true that there would probably have been at this day no British North American colonies had it not been for the immigration of the loyalists into Canada, there were, of course, before the Revolution, action and reaction between the old colonies and Quebec. Enmity had always existed. So well known are the untoward incidents both before and after the conquest of Quebec that it is needless to recall them. They were due to antagonisms of antipathetic types, and milder though they have become they still persist. No part of Canada would oppose more vehemently than Quebec any suggestion of absorption into the United States. Recently a Quebec Judge has written a charming series of sketches of peasant life in his province, and in one of these a boy asks his old uncle what he means by *La Patrie*. In answer he refers to the life and traditions of his people rooted in the soil, and afterwards as he knelt at prayer he glanced at his gun on the wall and murmured: "Oui! Je voudrais voir l'Américain qui viendrait prendre ma terre!—Au nom du Père, et du Fils et du Saint Esprit. Ainsi soit-il. Mettons nous en la presence de Dieu[1]." . . "Il faut savoir que, pour l'oncle Jean, l'ennemi, quel qu'il fût, c'était l'Américain."

The province is out of sympathy with American

[1] Judge Adjutor Rivard, *Chez Nous*, pp. 143, 141.

democracy. Even American Catholicism is too liberal for the Quebec ecclesiastic. Nor does the sentimental affinity of the educated American for modern France win over the French Canadian, for he disapproves the very ideals of France which America admires. The American glories in his progressiveness, the French-Canadian lives on the authority of tradition. The latter holds the former at arm's length as a menace to his security; to the former Quebec is a picturesque corner of medieval Europe in a bleak northland, delightful merely for a summer tour.

And yet for nearly a century Quebec has seen her sons drawn without ceasing by the lure of the United States, and the stream still flows across the border though in smaller volume. Emigration began as long ago as 1834, and from that time until the present the movement has been so great that there are now said to be, on good authority, not less than 1,750,000 people of French-Canadian origin in the United States, and according to the United States census 307,800 of them Canadian born. Nearly 75 per cent. are to be found in New England settled in solid blocks in the industrial towns such as Fall River, Lawrence, Lowell, New Bedford, Haverhill, Worcester, where they are employed especially in cotton and shoe factories. True to type, they have large families and they now constitute one-seventh of the population of New England; they have acquired great influence in some localities as they are naturally hard-working, thrifty, peaceful, and opposed to labour strikes. Though they are law-abiding citizens and all but a small percentage have become naturalized, the French-Canadians have been so far like an unassimilable deposit upon the soil of New England. They are the most conservative of all new-comers. Race, language, the mystical bonds of religion and tradition attach them to one another and to their kinsfolk on the banks of the St Lawrence, where lies their homeland spiritualized by the song, legend and labours of their fathers, consecrated by their piety and tradition. Even in New England the French-Canadian desires to keep not only his church, but his school and if possible his language. Will he be able to wrest these concessions from the politicians? If so, Quebec may reach down into New England and impose upon portions of that region a culture older than her own, as she has already done in the English-speaking eastern townships of the province and is now doing in some of the counties of New Brunswick and Ontario. There is, however, a counteractive influence at work in the efforts that are being put forth by many of the ecclesiastical and nationalist leaders to divert the tide of emigration into northern Ontario, and even to bring back home some of those who have crossed into New England. That these efforts have met with no little success may be inferred from the decided decrease during the last decade in the number of French Canadian-born residents of the United States, as shown by the census.

Notwithstanding this extension of Quebec into New England, the reciprocal influence of New England upon Quebec is almost negligible, apart from such transmission due to commercial establishments as is found in Montreal and in the shrinking English-speaking portions of the eastern townships.

If the wedge of Quebec were withdrawn, the Maritime provinces and Ontario would easily coalesce into a remarkably homogeneous population. Their origins are very similar; in the main a loyalist substratum with a superstructure of immigration from Great Britain. In Nova Scotia, however, there had been settlements from New England, the north of Ireland and Scotland before the American Revolution. Even the Canadian is apt to forget that within his own borders there is one community of white men which has existed for a longer time than any in the original English-speaking colonies. Port Royal, now the charming little town of Annapolis Royal in Nova Scotia, was founded in 1605, three years before Champlain first came to Quebec. Round its old fort were waged many battles between the French and the English, and long drawn out was the resistance of the Acadians. Francis Parkman has invested their history with romance, though he has also told it wit the accuracy of a scientific investigator. If his ancestors in New England joined in the attacks upon the French in Acadia, he has made noble amends by the way in which he has immortalized their story.

After the expulsion of the Acadians in 1755, their vacant farms were occupied by colonists from Massachusetts and Connecticut, and to this day there is to be found along the shores of Minas Basin and in the valleys of the Cornwallis and the Annapolis rivers in Nova Scotia a genuine bit of old New England. American fishermen also had settled on the rugged southern shores, and their descendants have names like those that are to-day familiar on Cape Cod. In all these parts a generation later "Sam Slick" found himself at home.

When the Revolution broke out these Americans caused no little anxiety to the British Government by reason of their restiveness and occasional uprisings stimulated by *agents provocateurs* from the rebellious colonies. They were under cross fires. Their revolting kinsfolk despised them for their apathy, and privateers and even ships of war ravaged their hamlets and destroyed their trade; the British forced the oath of allegiance upon them and constrained them to take up arms in the royal cause; but had it not been for the garrison in Halifax, Nova Scotia would probably have fallen to the New England states, so few were the English, Irish and Scottish inhabitants at that time. The importance of these settlements in the history of the Dominion lies not so much in the part that their descendants have played, as in their having formed a nucleus for the coming into being of English-speaking Canada. Had not Nova Scotia remained steadfast to Britain, whither could the loyalists have gone? How, then, would an English-speaking Canada have been created?

As has been already remarked, a common substratum of loyalism underlies the English-speaking population of Ontario and the Maritime provinces. It may, perhaps, be not too much to say that the loyalists have been the most influential element in the history of these provinces; at least in the order of time it has been so, for they were the founders of New Brunswick and of Upper Canada, and until this day the traditions of loyalism so pervade sections of eastern Canada that in some measure they determine the attitude of the country to the United States.

But loyalism has also left a permanent mark on the character of the American people. The persecution and extrusion of the loyalists reacted upon those who wronged them. Not only was a distinctive type of character with its ideals lost to the American democracy, but by the fault of human nature the American grew embittered against the injured exiles when he saw them struggling to their feet in a new home on his northern frontier, a nuisance, he believed, if not a danger, with which in time he would have to deal.

Loyalism came into being during the ten years that preceded the signing of the Declaration of Independence, and was not finally expelled from or absorbed into the new states until eight years after that event; but its origins are complex and go back for the better part of a century. They are to be found in the diverging types of character within the colonies themselves, and in incompatible political and religious ideals. Loyalism was no superficial movement, but was one of two deep currents which, when they met in full volume, made a troubled surface. This is not the place to discuss the effect of the Imperial policy of the eighteenth century, with its doctrine of mercantilism, nor of the natural consequence of such a policy in stimulating the independent trade of the colonial merchants; nor to enlarge upon the political theories that were engaging the earnest attention of the colonials. Long established differences in character were a powerful cause of estrangement. Unadulterated Englishmen though the Pilgrim Fathers and their successors who made New England were, their nearest of kin in England were not to be found among the governing classes of the eighteenth century. They had a natural antipathy to the Anglican clergy and to the English officials who gathered round the colonial governors, and as they moved into Pennsylvania and Virginia they diffused in these parts their dislikes or prejudices. Even Benjamin Franklin, a genial and representative character and a distinctive American, was radically different from his contemporary, Dr Samuel Johnson, who, as the late Sir Walter Raleigh said, "has almost become a tutelary genius of the English people . . . a conformist by principle . . . (who found it) good to be talked to by his Sovereign." He disliked Milton and was repelled by the Puritans of New England for their Whiggism. If Johnson and Franklin had got on well together it would have been because of their natural geniality. They were representatives of separating peoples.

But another not less potent cause in the creation of loyalism which led to disruption lay in the antagonism that had sprung up between the frontier and the prosperous towns on the Atlantic coast. Population had moved out of rugged New England into New York and Pennsylvania, and the frontier was becoming constantly more distant. On this borderland, as always, energetic people made their homes, whose comfort, in so far as it existed, depended upon their own hard work, and whose success bred not only self-confidence but hostility to the well-to-do in the older settlements. The farmer, the trader, the artizan, felt that he had many grievances against the rich merchant. It was, in one sense, the eternal antagonism between labour and capital, but more than that, it was the assertion of the frontier spirit against any kind of privilege. Conservatism is the natural product of inherited wealth, and entrenched comfort is always timid lest radicalism disturb it; and in this period of colonial history the danger was not unreal, as there was a widespread movement among the common people of the new settlements to take the power of government into their own hands. It was only what might have been expected that the wealthier merchants and large land-owners of New York and Pennsylvania should sympathize more with the Home Government than with the pestilential orders that were dominating the colonial assemblies[1]. Further, these elements of discontent were reinforced by aggrieved immigrants into Pennsylvania, Virginia and the southern colonies from the north of Ireland and Scotland, few of whom, either at home or in America, had sympathy with the authorities in the English Church or State. Such leading Americans as became loyalist saw with concern a new order arising and the radical taking control, and they asked themselves whither this undisciplined folk would carry them. Unfortunate men that they were, they had their own troubles with the Mother-Country, and with governors and officials. The mercantile system, the unwise proceedings of England in the Admiralty Courts, the Molasses Act, the Stamp Act, the stupidity of governors and the arrogance of army officers galled them. But for them England was more than

[1] See J. T. Adams, *Revolutionary New England,* pp. 100 ff.

her over-bearing or bungling government: she was the fountain-head of their principles in Church and State. Their loyalty, moreover, was kept alive by their aversion to those who were leading the country into rebellion. They clung to the hope, true American patriots as they claimed to be, that the troubles would be settled without an appeal to arms, and they urged the Home authorities not to send out troops. But after Lexington the die was cast, the hope of a peaceful settlement was dissipated and the loyalists then took up the gage of battle and entered desperately into a civil war. Hitherto there had been a moderate party, but when once the appeal was made to arms the moderate was suspected of being a concealed and therefore a treacherous enemy. Fear ministered fuel, and all loyalists were made to suffer grievously: confiscation of property, personal indignities, rough handling by the mob, tarring and feathering, even murders, make up the story of their woes.

There was, of course, reason for this fear, because the loyalist element was very large, especially in the states of New York and Pennsylvania. It has been estimated that in New York state, out of a population of 185,000 quite 90,000 were loyalist, and that two-thirds of the property in the city and suburbs of New York belonged to the "Tories"; therefore the British never bombarded it. In 1777 Washington, almost in despair because of the disaffection of his troops, wrote, "If America fall it will be by the death thrust of the loyalist rather than by the British."

After our experience of the Great War it is less difficult to understand the action of the American revolutionist. When hostilities are unloosed, neutrality must hide itself; the more desperate affairs become the more do human passions rage. The revolutionist had no difficulty in persuading himself that he was fighting for the ideal of basal human rights which he tried to express in the Declaration of Independence, and again and again he realized that because of the presence of the loyalists the issue was hanging in the balance. In his eyes they were both traitors and fools, and therefore he treated them with cruelty and scorn.

Though loyalists were found in all classes, their leaders came chiefly from the landed proprietors of New York and Pennsylvania and the rich merchants of the sea-board cities. The high officials and most of those who, whether propertied or as serving folk, had been taught in the Anglican prayer-book to reverence the King's Majesty remained loyal to the British cause. The old Puritan of New England and the Presbyterian Whig of Pennsylvania and Virginia made the backbone of the Revolution.

As the fortunes of the British waned emigration began. Many of the wealthiest fled to England, and others took refuge in New York as their last stronghold. Thereupon all their property, real and personal, was confiscated and sold for the benefit of the State. Two results followed from the action of the Americans towards the loyalists. The first was that their expulsion eradicated not only a type of character but a land system. Large estates were broken up into small holdings. Remembering how dangerously influential against their cause the former leaders of that feudal and commercial society had been, the revolting colonists were determined that never again would they have a chance to overthrow the young democracy. Therefore the lands were divided among new owners who held different political views. It is true that after peace was declared large numbers who had been loyalist in sympathy quietly accepted the inevitable, perhaps as many as 55,000 remaining in New York State alone; but it may be said with truth that the conservative element had disappeared[1].

This explains in part the repudiation by the several states of the clause in the treaty of 1783 for the indemnification of the loyalists for their losses. It was stipulated that the Congress of the United States should earnestly recommend the several states to restore the rights and possessions of "real British subjects" and of such loyalists as had not borne arms against their countrymen. All others were to be allowed to recover their property on payment of the

[1] Cf. Flick, *Loyalism in New York*, p. 158.

sale price within six months; confiscations were to cease, hostilities to be abandoned. But the terms of the treaty were not fulfilled; the states repudiated what was almost an engagement of Congress; harshness continued and the young Republic went forth upon its way having violated the first treaty that had been made on its behalf.

The second result of the expulsion by the Americans of the loyalists was the creation of a new people on their northern border. Had they treated them with decency it is probable that most of them would have found their way back to their old localities, and the new British provinces would have developed slowly and without the inveterate nucleus round which their character took its shape. But having wronged the loyalist, the American himself continued bitter towards him and treated his sufferings with sarcasm, nor did the 40,000 exiles in the northern wilderness forget their treatment. Contempt was mutual and had not died out before once more war fanned it into flame in 1812.

Thousands of these exiles were thrown upon the rugged shores of Nova Scotia, thousands more landed at the mouth of the St John river; and thousands of others worked their way into Canada by the St Lawrence, or from New York round the east and west ends of Lake Ontario into what is now the province of that name. The story of Shelburne, Nova Scotia, seems to-day like the unsubstantial fabric of a vision. For a few years towards the end of the eighteenth century it was a gay city, set in a wilderness of rocks and forests and sustained by the British Government. To-day it is a quiet little town with only well laid out streets to tell of its hectic prosperity.

Some 35,000 loyalists entered the eastern province and 5,000 came into Canada, the former chiefly from New York city and New England, the latter from upper New York state and Pennsylvania. They were of all sorts and conditions. Social rank and official position were observed in making grants of land, larger areas and also lucrative posts being given to officers and those of higher station. Most of the wealthier loyalists escaped to England, but some persons of distinction came to the provinces. Among those attainted in New York was the Rev. Charles Inglis, rector of Trinity church, and later first bishop of Nova Scotia, and Beverley Robinson, a name well known in Virginian and in Canadian history. Writing to the Archbishop of Canterbury in 1787, Inglis says that some of the principal members of the House of Assembly of Nova Scotia were his old friends; and in Fredericton, New Brunswick, in 1785 a memorial for the establishment of an Academy of liberal arts and sciences was signed by two graduates of Harvard, a son of a former governor of Rhode Island, an eminent Quaker merchant of Boston, a physician born in Boston, and a

Bostonian who had served as a general in the Army[1]. Also the earliest outstanding personage in Canada was Sir John Johnson, son of Sir William Johnson, who before the war possessed immense estates in the Mohawk valley. He became the leading colonial military figure, and with him were many officers. As time went by, those who had been leaders in the old colonies naturally gathered about the Governor and took political control. It held true of them, as a generation later of Haliburton's "Old Judge,"— "In religion he is a churchman and in politics a conservative, as is almost every gentleman in these colonies." Having sacrificed greatly for the royal cause they felt that they had a right to privilege, and that the safety and welfare of the provinces depended upon them; so they sought to reproduce in the northern wilderness institutions similar to those to which they had been accustomed. But by far the largest number of the loyalists were people of comparatively humble origin, some even illiterate; farmers and artizans, together with regiments of soldiers disbanded at the close of the war. The common folk who came by land brought their household goods and stock with them, though for some time they put dependence upon the British Government for their supplies of tools, seeds and provisions.

[1] W. O. Raymond, *The Genesis of the University of New Brunswick*, p. 1.

It is not our purpose to trace the rise of discontent among the common people, nor the steps of the struggle which in the time issued in responsible government. Whatever were their domestic troubles, all parties in the first generation were united in their fear of and opposition to the rebel American.

Loyalism was only one, if the most important, phase of American immigration into eastern Canada. John Graves Simcoe, Lieutenant-Governor of Upper Canada from 1791–5 desired to get his province well populated, and being persuaded that many Americans were still loyal at heart he let it be known in the United States that such settlers would be welcome to make homes for themselves in Upper Canada. Many accepted the invitation and proved to be, in general, a quiet and hard working class, but among them were land-seekers such as float like scum on the top of every wave of immigration; others of them were adventurers hoping to make profit when, as they expected, Upper Canada, like Texas in later days, would fall into the United States. That these undesirables were no inconsiderable element in the population is shown in a letter of Governor Gore's in 1808: "Excepting the inhabitants of Glengarry and those persons who have served in the American war and their descendants, who form a considerable body of men, the residue of the inhabitants of this Colony consist chiefly of persons who have emigrated from the States of America and of consequence retain those ideas of equality and insubordination, much to the prejudice of this Government, so prevalent in that country[1]." Also as late as 1822 Lord Dalhousie favoured the French Canadians of the lower province as a make-weight against Americanizing tendencies which he discerned in Upper Canada; and under a ruling given by the Imperial authorities in 1824 American citizens were not allowed to hold or inherit real estate, but this led to hardship on such a large body of settlers that in 1828 the legislature of Upper Canada passed a special Act conferring civil rights and the privileges of British subjects on many of them. The picture of her American neighbours in 1832 given by Mrs Moodie in *Roughing it in the Bush* shows thriftless, rude folk with ignorant contempt of the English such as were met with at that time in the frontier settlements of western New York. This, however, cannot be taken as true of the average in better parts of the province, though in the period of troubles which led up to the Rebellion of 1837 complaint was often made by the loyalists of the large number of American settlers who clung to republican principles and favoured the radical views of the "Reformers."

It has been already remarked that in the English-speaking portions of eastern Canada a stratum of

[1] Sir Charles Lucas, *The Canadian War of* 1812, p. 16.

British immigration was deposited on the earlier loyalist layer, and that from these two has been derived the Canadian of Ontario and the Maritime provinces. Shipload after shipload of people in never-ending procession from Britain was landed in the first half of the nineteenth century, till by 1851 the population of Canada had grown to 952,000, of whom 526,000 were non-French Canadian born. Most of the increase was due to the English, Scotch and Irish, though 44,000 hailed from the United States. Much of the immigration, especially such as was directed by Talbot, Selkirk, Galt and the Canada Land Company was excellent in quality, but unfortunately thousands of the very poor whom Britain wished to get rid of by state-aided emigration were landed penniless and remained long in destitution. Between 1825 and 1847 the United States got a great deal of British emigration which was, on the average, of better quality than that which came to Canada. They would not accept paupers, but offered opportunity to the thrifty with a little capital, and to skilled labourers, who therefore found their way into their new lands. Sad though the chapters of immigration so often are, the best British immigrant to Canada, sturdy, honest and courageous, triumphed over his difficulties, and old Ontario bears witness to his character. Comparatively few were farmers; there were artizans, shop-keepers, miners and soldiers who knew little or nothing about

the land, and many were the instances of pathetic mal-
adjustment; but most of the new-comers had no
grievances against Britain which they still thought of as
home, and living by themselves, confined to their settlements, they preserved amidst their hardships their old
traditions, and for a generation continued to be a bit
of the old land in the wilds of the new.

When transplanted to the environment of Canada,
the Briton took on superficially such new features,
not unlike those of the American, as might arise
from similar life on the frontier and from neighbourly
contacts. But his character, as well as his sympathies,
remained British. Many were radicals from the industrial centres of England, and they naturally
adopted the reform views of those who preceded
them, but this did not mean any reinforcement of
annexation sentiment. In fact, the new-comers were
more unlike the Americans than were the loyalists,
and not even the American school-master who often
appeared in the clearings and villages, changed their
point of view. British immigration overwhelmed
American influences in Ontario, and superimposed
upon the loyalist substratum it has made that province steadfast for British connection. But a new type
has been produced, the result of the new conditions
in which the old stock found itself.

A returning ebb of population from Canada into
the United States began in the thirties from Quebec

and in the forties from English-speaking Canada, and that flow has continued until the present. Not only did thousands of poor immigrants who had come from Ireland cross to the United States between 1840 and 1850, but many of the best, who, finding the country in a depressed condition and being disappointed with their opportunities, moved on to the United States and became an important element in their population. In 1850 Canadians formed 6·6 per cent. of the foreigners in the United States, and since that time probably two millions, or somewhat less than half the natural increase of Canada during the same period, have become domiciled south of the border. The American census of 1920 enumerated about 1,117,000 Canadians then living in the United States, of whom 810,000 were non-French. According to the same census the Canadian immigration was about equal to that from the British Isles, slightly larger than that from Ireland, and equal to that from Poland. As has been already remarked, the overwhelming number of the French-Canadians are found in New England. The Maritime provinces send their quota also into New England; Ontario sends hers chiefly into the larger cities of New York, Ohio, Michigan and Illinois; the Western provinces send theirs to the states on the Pacific coast, which also receive many from all the provinces. Probably no one state has contributed so largely as Ontario to New

York, Michigan and Illinois. The cities of Detroit, Boston, Chicago, Buffalo and Los Angeles contain relatively to the native-born Americans of English-speaking origin a large proportion of Canadians. In the city of New York there are more Canadians, other than those of French extraction, than Scotch or French, and nearly as many as Norwegians, Czecko-Slovaks or Swedes.

For three generations the people of the Maritime provinces, of Quebec and of Ontario have with dis-tress beheld tens of thousands of their most vigorous sons and daughters pass over the border. It is now an old but sad story; for so often those who have gone are among the best of the stock, the adventurous sons and daughters of those who left Britain, the kinsfolk of those who helped to build the Empire. Canadians are not a restless people; they have left home with regret and have gone in order to make a living. Canada lies alongside a rich country, in which revival of trade shows itself earlier and which recovers from depression, as a rule, a year or two sooner. When work is plentiful abroad and scarce at home the volume of emigration swells rapidly. Since the War the exodus has been large, as the material prosperity of the United States has been much greater than that of Canada. Moreover the native-born Canadian is exempted from the quota regulations that are applied to other new-comers.

None of the peoples who throw in their lot with the Americans so easily adapt themselves to their life as Canadians. They become loyal to their new home and are not regarded as aliens, though many do not undergo naturalization. Men and women of every calling have taken their place in the movement— graduates of universities, school-teachers, actuaries, nurses, traders, artizans—and by the faithful discharge of their duties not a few have reached positions of high honour. They compel respect for the people from whom they come, and they have made a good name for their country. In turn these expatriated Canadians have become agents of good-will among their old friends, and on their visits home they create a kindlier spirit in their relatives towards the neighbour who has received them so hospitably; wherefore out of the sorrows of the emigrant a better spirit is being born.

At no time since the early decades of the nineteenth century have many Americans made their homes in eastern Canada. In 1871 there were only 64,500 in the whole Dominion, and in the last twenty years such as have come to Ontario, Quebec and the Maritime provinces have been for the most part agents or employees of manufacturing firms which have established plants in order to compete more favourably under tariff conditions for Canadian or British trade. But according to the census of 1921 there were

374,000 American-born residents of Canada, and during the previous decade there had been an immigration of 1,366,000 Americans into Canada, a large number of whom, however, were naturalized citizens of the United States.

This rapid increase was due to their discovery of the Canadian North-West. The federation of the four provinces in 1867 was only made possible by the belief that the West would soon belong to them, and the Dominion virtually came into being as it was occupied. Within the memory of many who are still alive the West was the "great lone land" with small groups of people at far separated places, and traversed only by the Indian, the French Metis, the servants of the Hudson's Bay Company and a few adventurers. Though there had been a settlement on the Red River for many years, it was not until the middle of the century that the Canadian, realizing that the country might be of immense importance to his own future, resolved to penetrate the mystery which dwelt in the silence of the regions beyond, and like the American confronting his own West two generations earlier to become the master of those vast unknown spaces. Unknown they were because the Hudson's Bay Company had kept a jealous guard over their preserves lest they should be invaded by the agricultural settler who would injure their trade in furs, though incidentally the West was saved thereby for

Canada as the American was kept out. No country has had more intrepid explorers than Mackenzie, Fraser and Thompson, but they worked for the fur companies, and immigration did not follow on their trails. It was men from Ontario who opened up and first took possession of the prairies, and laid the foundations of ordered society, and that in the face of opposition, for not until after ten or fifteen years of effort did Canada succeed in getting control of the western territories from the Hudson's Bay Company in 1869 for £300,000. How difficult the negotiations were, the blunders made in the transfer and the political troubles that issued in the first rebellion of French half-breeds under Riel, form a well-known chapter in the history of the West. When the tumults were allayed immigrants from Canada began to enter Manitoba by the Red River. It was an arduous journey to a rigorous climate, which none but the brave would face. But with the construction of the Canadian Pacific Railway the population increased rapidly along its lines, and until this day the Canadians from Ontario are to be found, generally speaking, within the sphere of that system. In the eighties it almost seemed as though some counties of Ontario, such as Huron and Bruce, had emptied themselves upon the prairies. The flow from the eastern provinces into the United States was stayed, being diverted into the West. Not only the pick of the young farmers from the East, but teachers, clergymen, physicians and lawyers, among them some of the most distinguished graduates of Canadian universities, sought their fortunes in the new land. Government was established on eastern lines, schools were modelled on those of Ontario, the churches followed the settlers and conducted vigorous home missions, and eastern banks dotted the prairies with their branches. The country never got out of hand; troubles with the Indians were few; the criminal population was very small; law and order were enforced from the beginning by swift and evenly distributed justice which was carried out by the North-West Mounted Police, whose fame has gone throughout the English-speaking world. Canadians not only laid the foundations of the West, but they have erected the largest portion of its superstructure, though English and Scottish settlers also came in early and shared with them in establishing the institutions of society.

At the World's Fair in Chicago in 1893, the advantages of the Canadian prairies were well advertised, and five or six years later a movement began from the United States into the western provinces. By skilful publicity and offers of free grants of good land the small stream rose at the opening of the twentieth century to considerable proportions, and rapidly for the six years previous to 1913 when it reached its height at 139,000 immigrants. After the policy of making free land grants was withdrawn the flow slackened, and the War reduced it to a trickle. But in the last few years the stream has begun to rise again and it will probably increase if the present hopes of prosperity are realised. More than 100,000 American families, usually of good quality and useful farming experience, entered those provinces before the War. Of these Saskatchewan received the largest number, which nearly equalled the Canadian homesteaders and was twice as great as that of all other non-Canadians. Manitoba got fewest. As a rule they took land on the railways that run north and south and on the east and west lines that are now incorporated in the Canadian National system. They have come from the states of North Dakota, Minnesota, and Washington, and, in lesser numbers, from Iowa, Illinois, Michigan; even from New York and Massachusetts. One-third of the immigration, especially of those whose homes were on the American prairie, was probably of north European stock—Swedish and Norwegian; another third was of the eastern American stock, descendants of those who three generations ago set out for the valley of the Mississippi; the last third consisted of former Canadians and Britons repatriating themselves from many states, some belonging to the first but many to the second generation. As the price of land rose in the United States and high capitalization reduced the profits of farm products, they sold out, often to Americans moving from the eastern states, and began life anew on the Canadian prairies.

These people have made remarkably good citizens. In a very true sense it may be said that if eastern Canadians discovered the West, the Americans have opened the eyes of the western Canadian to the possibilities of his own country, especially on the material side. They are excellent farmers, understanding how to make the most of their land, and having brought with them the secret of the successful cultivation of the drier portions of the prairies. They are alert and shrewd in business, with an eye to money-making whether by trading in land, booming real estate, pushing the sale of farm implements, developing the lumber industry or advertising oil prospects. They show their initiative and common sense by their use of labour-saving devices and practical conveniences on the farm and in the house. In fact, the frontier characteristics so well known in the American West naturally repeat themselves on the Canadian prairies. In so far as these people have made permanent homes for themselves they have not exploited the land for their own advantage, but have become excellent Canadians, accepting the new order of things and the new institutions and endeavouring to take their share in working them.

Good feeling exists in the Prairie provinces between the older Canadian and the American, unless here and there some prejudice crops up where loyalists or recent English arrivals have settled. The action of the American in the West during the War occasioned no serious criticism. It is true that he did not respond so quickly as the British who leaped at once to the need of the Mother-land and led in enlistment; nor did he come up to the Canadian-born who made a good second; but he played a reasonable part. Hitherto he had known nothing of the outside world. "Iowa" meant more to him than all Europe, and it was difficult for a man who had never seen the ocean to realize for the first time that duty was calling him to cross it in defence of an ideal. But go he did, and that too long before his relatives south of the line had been persuaded that they must throw in their weight against Germany.

This American has learned much about Britain and to respect British institutions as they have been reproduced in Canada, and so he may be a useful interpreter of them to his folk across the border. Of eastern Canada, however, he knows little and is out of sympathy with much that he hears about it. In fact a very acute observer has remarked that "in many ways we stand much nearer to the rural life of the northern middle states than we do to the urban life of eastern Canada." But the American immigrant has become a friend to the western Canadian, and shows no sign of using this friendship to undermine his loyalty to the Dominion.

British Columbia, isolated from the East by her mountains, has had her own history and preserves her own individuality, but her incoming was necessary for the completion of the Dominion. When in 1871 Confederation was accepted by the people as a guarantee of their future, it was brought about chiefly through the influence of the few Canadians who had made leading positions for themselves on the Coast. The British-born and the Americans, who were in the majority, were not on the whole favourably disposed to it. In earlier years the population had come in by sea or through the United States. After the decision as to the Oregon boundary, the Hudson's Bay Company transferred its headquarters to Victoria on Vancouver Island, and for years little was known of the mainland. Fortunately the head of the Company, who was also the governor of Vancouver Island and afterwards also of the mainland, Sir James Douglas, was a man of unusual character and ability, with autocratic tendencies which, on the whole, led to good government. But growth was very slow. About Victoria the dominating influences came from the Hudson's Bay employees. With the discovery of gold in the Fraser river, however, the whole situation changed. People poured in from everywhere, most of them Americans. But owing to the fluctuations of the gold prospects, the numbers rose and fell, and it was not until the province was linked with the East by the Canadian Pacific Railway that the growth went ahead with any degree of permanency.

Of all the provinces British Columbia is that in which the British-born element bears the greatest proportion to the total population, that is to say 30.6 per cent., and Victoria is the most English city in the Dominion. About 45 per cent. of the people of the province are of Canadian stock and 10 per cent. American. This American influence has been felt in the mining and the lumbering districts, especially on the mainland. Though the political ties of the province are strongly British and it is now genuinely an organic part of Canada, the commercial and social relationships with Seattle, Portland and California are numerous and strong. This is due to the conditions imposed by geography. In many respects the Pacific coast is one. Movement is easily made north and south; towards the east it must be through mountains and across wide prairies. This coast also faces the Far East as a unit, and the attitude towards Oriental immigration is the same from British Columbia to California.

From this survey of the population of the Dominion it is obvious that the unifying of the provinces into a national life has been a process of extreme difficulty.

Confederation itself was a remarkable accomplishment. A sense of national unity does exist, but it has had to surmount great obstacles, geographical, racial and economic. The United States was given a much easier problem in the attainment of unity, though Canada has never had to meet anything like the slavery question and the Civil War, nor has she yet had to assimilate vast hordes of immigrants chiefly from south and south-eastern Europe with their new and perplexing difficulties; relatively however the loss of many of her best people through emigration has been much greater.

In the large elements of population so alike in character which are found in the dominant portion of the United States and in English-speaking Canada lies the possibility of a real understanding between these two countries. An analysis of the distinctive and the similar features of the life and thought of both will substantiate this judgment. Hitherto, however, the process of good understanding has often been inhibited by inherited dislikes and prejudices, which have been stimulated and renewed by disagreements over undetermined boundaries, by political antagonisms and by clashing interests in trade. These, therefore, will be considered in succession.

CHAPTER II

The Determining of the Boundaries

A<small>N</small> undetermined frontier is a fertile source of trouble; not so much because of the value of the disputed territory as of the claim that it is national property. What the nation has it will hold; sentiment adds strength to the grasp; even to sell may appear an unworthy compromise in a young country. As long, therefore, as the boundaries between the United States and Canada were anywhere in dispute, a local irritation might have quickly developed into widespread inflammatory disorder. So dangerous were many of these unresolved problems that Americans and Canadians may well be thankful that they have been honourably settled, and are to-day incidents of history which rarely excite hostile comment on either side.

The fixing of the boundaries began in 1783 and was not concluded until 1908, and though there were during the negotiations one or two instances of local uprisings between the settlers on both sides of the line, the final issue was in no case due to a display of force. That such difficult matters should have been brought to a conclusion by reasonable negotiation is a great tribute to the character of those whose interests were concerned; all the greater because there are so few natural barriers as obstacles in the path of adventurers who in their haste to occupy tempting territory interpret the indefinite to their own advantage. Human nature and the countries being what they are, it is remarkable that the peace was not broken; indeed on one or two occasions the issue was accepted because England was bound that frontier matters should not end in hostilities. What would have happened had Canada always demanded to settle them for herself it is unsafe to surmise. Though she was dissatisfied with England on some occasions for what she agreed to on her behalf, probably she could not have done any better in the interpretation of treaties that had been made before she came into existence. In several of the most important cases the real cause of trouble was to be found in the ignorance or possibly the carelessness of the original negotiators.

This is especially true in respect of the settlement of the boundary between Maine, New Brunswick and Quebec, which is the oldest, the most famous and was for long the most dangerous of all frontier disputes. Even at present the Canadian, when taking the shortest route from Montreal to St John he must cross the state of Maine for some three hundred miles, speaks with disappointment of Ashburton's irreparable concession to the United States. But Lord Ash-

burton has been unjustly blamed. The balance of
expert opinion is in his favour on the ground that he
made the best of a bad bargain for Great Britain.
That bargain was embodied in the Treaty of 1783
when the victorious Americans took every advantage
of their success, though it must be pleaded in ex-
tenuation for the British negotiators that the only
maps they had of that unexplored territory were
faulty. If it is realized that even as late as 1838 roads
had not yet been built from Maine into the disputed
territory, and that the Americans had to ask from New
Brunswick the privilege of allowing their surveyors
to pass through that province in order to carry out
their work in the northern part of the state, the ignorance of the original negotiators, deplorable though
the results have been to Canada, is explicable. But
when once the interpretation of the treaty began it
was conducted by lawyers of first class ability. Britain
chose men of the province affected who were deeply
interested in the decision, and the sustained skill of
her diplomacy finally won for her a comparatively
favourable judgment.

The portion of the second article of the treaty of
1783 dealing with the eastern boundary is as follows:

And that all disputes which might arise in future on the
subject of the boundaries of the said United States may be
prevented, it is hereby agreed and declared that the following
are and shall be their boundaries, viz.: from the North-West

angle of Nova Scotia, viz.: that angle which is formed by a line drawn due north from the source of the St Croix River to the Highlands; along the said Highlands which divide those rivers which empty themselves into the River St Lawrence from those which fall into the Atlantic Ocean to the North-Westernmost head of the Connecticut River, down along the middle of that river to the forty-fifth degree of north latitude; from thence by a line due West on said latitude until it strikes the River Iroquois or Cataraquy; thence down along the middle of that River into Lake Ontario....East, by a line to be drawn along the middle of the River St Croix from its mouth in the Bay of Fundy to its source, and from its source directly North to the aforesaid Highlands, which divide the rivers which fall into the Atlantic Ocean from those which fall into the River St Lawrence: comprehending all islands within twenty leagues of any shores of the United States, and lying between lines to be drawn due East from the points where the aforesaid boundaries between Nova Scotia on the one part, and East Florida on the other, shall respectively touch the Bay of Fundy and the Atlantic Ocean; excepting such islands as now are, or heretofore have been, within the limits of the said Province of Nova Scotia.

Three main issues were involved in this section of the treaty: (*a*) What river was truly intended under the name of the river St Croix? (*b*) What islands in the Bay of Passamaquoddy belonged to His Britannic Majesty and what to the United States? and (*c*) What was meant by "the North-West angle of Nova Scotia"?

The first issue was decided by a Commission in 1798; the second by a Commission with the same

British Commissioner, Thomas Barclay, of New Brunswick, in 1817; the third by direct negotiation between Daniel Webster, American Secretary of State, and Lord Ashburton, in 1842.

The treaty of 1783 was intended to perpetuate the accepted boundaries between the colony of Massachusetts Bay, then including what is now the state of Maine, and Nova Scotia, then including what is now the province of New Brunswick. The boundaries of Massachusetts Bay were defined in the charter given by William and Mary; those of Nova Scotia were outlined in the charter given to Sir William Alexander in 1621, and were more fully detailed, though with an unfortunate change, in the commission issued in 1763 to Wilmot as governor of Nova Scotia. Three of the American framers of the treaty, John Adams, Jay and Franklin, survived until the first commission was appointed, but they could state nothing decisive as to its intention beyond the principle just referred to, except that Adams affirmed that the St Croix river was chosen because it was the eastern boundary of Massachusetts Bay. But unfortunately, Mitchell's map of 1755, on which the negotiators had traced the accepted boundaries, had disappeared and was never afterwards produced.

(*a*) The question for the first commission, that of 1798, to decide, was: What was the historical St Croix river? Historical because De Monts wintered there with his expedition in 1604, as described by Lescarbot and Champlain. Some of the Americans sought to identify it with the St John, though they made a stronger claim for a small stream flowing into the Bay of Fundy near what is now the village of St George. The British claimed the present St Croix, at the mouth of which the beautiful summer resort of St Andrews is situated. Their claim was upheld, and it was verified by the discovery of the remains of the fort and the winter encampment of De Monts on Dochet Island in the St Croix river. But the source of the St Croix was still to be determined, and as it had at least two branches, there was room for difference of opinion. The commmissioners, by a compromise, decided upon the large eastern branch, and thereby Britain gained on the whole in regard to territory.

(*b*) The Islands in Passamaquoddy Bay. The St Croix river empties into this bay, and in its mouth and off shore there lie a number of small islands, and two—Grand Manan, nine miles from the main coast, and Campobello—which are of great importance strategically. The former, visited and named by Champlain in 1604, is some twenty miles by five, richly timbered, with safe harbours and good fishing. Geographically these islands belong to Maine as being far within "twenty leagues of the United States," the limit given in the treaty, but the repre-

sentatives of Great Britain before the Commission of
1817 set forth that they had always been a part of
Nova Scotia and that the State of Massachusetts had
never claimed them until after 1783. The Commission accepted this view, and determined that all
the islands in Passamaquoddy Bay, except three small
ones which gave the United States protected access
to the river St Croix, belonged to His Britannic
Majesty. It was by reason of the skill with which her
case was presented that New Brunswick fared so well
at this tribunal.

(c) The third question was: What was meant by
"The North West angle of Nova Scotia"? This was
by far the most difficult, and was not answered until
after several fruitless negotiations and dangerous
collisions had taken place.

As the War of 1812-4 was drawing to a close,
the legislature of New Brunswick petitioned Great
Britain "to alter the boundaries between these states
(the U.S.A.) and this province, so as that the important line of communication between this and the
neighbouring province of Lower Canada by the river
St John may not be interrupted." This was from the
beginning a vital principle in all negotiations. If the
provinces of British North America were to have any
unity they must have means of intercommunication.
This holds to-day as much as ever. Unfortunately,
however, the Treaty of Ghent in 1814 left matters as

they were, except for the provision that a commission should be created to determine "the North-West angle of Nova Scotia." Two new features, however, had entered into the situation: in 1820 the province of Maine was erected into a separate state, and with its new dignity it grew more insistent that its claims should be upheld at Washington; it was also discovered that the British were in possession of a part of the disputed territory, the survey of the country made by order of the Joint Commission in 1817–18 having brought out to the surprise of the Americans the fact that certain Acadians forming the Madawaska settlement had their homes beyond the contested boundary. These people had received grants as early as 1783 on the upper St John, and had never been challenged by the United States.

When the Commission issued its decisions in 1821 the opinions of the two parties were found to be irreconcilable. The representatives differed absolutely as to the meaning and locality of the "highlands" reached by a line drawn due north from the source of the St Croix and separating the rivers flowing into the St Lawrence from those flowing into the Atlantic Ocean. Barclay, the British commissioner, claimed that the "highlands" were to be identified with Mars Hill, distant forty miles north of the source of the St Croix and about thirty-seven miles south of the St John river. This would have given New Brunswick some of the best parts of the present state of Maine. On the other hand the Americans decided upon a point sixty-six miles north of the St John, the result of which would have been almost to cut off communication between New Brunswick and Quebec, plainly against the spirit of the preamble of the treaty which was "upon the ground of reciprocal advantages and mutual convenience ...... (to) promote and secure to both perpetual peace and harmony."

The surveyors could find no such "highlands" as they were looking for, and Mitchell's map was of no use to the negotiators. Both at this time and until the conclusion of the whole matter the same two questions constantly recurred: What was meant by "highlands" and by "the Atlantic Ocean"? If the former term implied a mountainous region the British case was strengthened and the "North-West angle of Nova Scotia" would then come in central Maine; if it meant the higher ground or watershed separating the two river systems the American view was reinforced. How doubtful the question was is shown by the admission of the American commissioner Sullivan in a letter to President Madison that the British were right in interpreting "highlands" as a range of mountains. But this concession was afterwards abandoned.

In regard to the term "Atlantic Ocean" the commissioners were equally irreconcilable. The Americans held that it included not merely the Bay of Fundy, and that therefore the St John emptied into the Atlantic Ocean, but also the Gulf of St Lawrence, and that therefore the Restigouche river, which empties into Chaleur Bay, an inlet of the Gulf, in accordance with the treaty flowed into the Atlantic Ocean. The British were just as insistent that neither the Bay of Fundy nor much less Chaleur Bay could be called "the Atlantic Ocean." The Americans on their interpretation carried the line far north to the watershed where the Restigouche has its source; the British found the highlands in central Maine in which the rivers west of the St Croix which flow into the Atlantic take their rise. The British claimed that their interpretation had never changed since the determination of the boundaries of Quebec in 1763. So there was a deadlock, but settlers kept moving into the disputed areas and frequently causes of trouble arose which at any time might have become acute.

After further fruitless negotiations, in 1827 the two sides agreed to refer the case for judgment to the King of the Netherlands, who based the decision which he made in 1831 on a most thorough investigation. He could not arrive at a conclusion on the words of the treaty or the maps, and therefore gave a compromise judgment. A line was to be drawn due north from the source of the St Croix to the middle of the channel of the St John: thence the middle of the Channel of that river ascending it to the point where the river St Francis empties itself into the St John; thence the middle of the channel of the river St Francis, ascending it to the source of its south-westernmost branch: thence a line drawn due west to the point where it unites with the line claimed by the United States of America.

This award, though it gave the United States the larger portion of the territory, provided the British with the essential communication between Quebec and New Brunswick by the St John river. But Maine would not agree, and though the President was inclined to recommend its approval the Senate rejected the decision.

Difficulties soon reappeared, culminating in the serious "Restook War" in 1838-9, which assumed such proportions that the legislature of Maine placed eight hundred thousand dollars at the disposal of the Governor for military defence, and the President was authorized by Congress to call out the militia. Hostilities were held off only by skilful and influential mediation. Moved by the acute danger, Daniel Webster, then Secretary of State, himself initiated in 1841 direct negotiation with the British Government. Lord Ashburton was sent out in 1842 as a plenipotentiary. His experience in public affairs and his relations with American business men made him an excellent negotiator for the matter in hand, and he and Webster came to an agreement. By this the essential features of the award of the King of the Netherlands were confirmed, though the state of Maine received about nine hundred square miles less of territory; but access to the sea by the St John river was conceded to her lumbermen and farmers on the same terms as the inhabitants of New Brunswick enjoyed. Webster faced great difficulties in getting their agreement through the Senate, and sugar-coated the pill with a vote of two hundred and fifty thousand dollars to Maine and of fifty thousand dollars to Massachusetts.

Here comes in the episode that has been called "the Battle of the Maps." Unfortunately there never was a map attached to the treaty of 1783, and that of Mitchell used by the negotiators had disappeared. But shortly before the Webster-Ashburton negotiations began an American had discovered in Paris a map which he assumed had been sent by Franklin to the Comte de Vergennes, on which a red line was traced south of the St John river, presumably giving Britain a large portion of Maine. As a matter of fact the British knew about it, but Sir Robert Peel said in Parliament in 1843 that they had been unable to trace any connection between it and the dispatch sent by Dr Franklin to the French Count. However Webster probably believed it to be genuine, and he showed it discreetly to members of the Senate to persuade them of the value of his award.

Several other maps were used, one of which, found in the British Museum, with a red line traced by Oswald who negotiated the treaty of 1783, was of some importance in the discussion in the English Parliament as showing that Ashburton had done well for England. But the final decision was not determined by the maps, and "Ashburton is reported to have said that the maps were not made public at the time or the treaty would never have been effected[1]."

The rest of the award may be quickly dealt with. A survey made in 1818 had proved that an error had been made in drawing the boundary line which was supposed to be the 45th degree of latitude running from the "highlands" to the river St Lawrence. The Americans had erected fortifications, at great expense, at Rouse's Point which were found on the new survey to be within British territory. The Ashburton-Webster treaty confirmed the "old line," thus validating the property rights which had been granted by the respective governments, and the states of Vermont and New York gained a more important piece of land than fell to the British provinces in the much larger territorial concession made by Maine.

The treaty was received at the time with violent criticism in the United States, the British provinces and Great Britain. Each side insisted that its rights had been sacrificed, and to this day in Canada Ash-

[1] Hon. J. W. Foster, *A Century of American Diplomacy*, p. 286.

burton usually comes in for censure. But the preceding recital is sufficient, it is hoped, to show that he deserves a better reputation; inherited prejudices should yield to the opinion of impartial experts. If New Brunswick lost a portion of Maine through the ignorance of officials it was not Ashburton's fault; it may have been due to a change in the wording of the commission given to Wilmot as governor of Nova Scotia in 1763, in which the boundaries of that province were defined as a line running "due north" from the source of the St Croix river, whereas in the original grant to Sir William Alexander in 1621 they were described as "an imaginary straight line which is conceived to extend over the land or to run northward to the nearest bay, river or stream emptying into the Great River of Canada[1]." Another token of the weakness of the extreme claim made by New Brunswick is found in her later action, when in her controversy with Quebec on the boundary her representatives put forth some of the same arguments that had been employed formerly by the United States.

This question has been dealt with at some length not only because it issued in what Mr Root has called "the most important treaty that has ever been made to preserve peace between Great Britain and the United States in settling the boundaries," but be-

[1] James White, *Canada and its Provinces*, VIII, pp. 756–764.

cause it is an example of those not infrequent traditions which are a source of lingering irritation long after the international differences have been settled on reasonable terms.

Another portion of Article II of the treaty of 1783, already quoted, runs as follows: from where the 45th degree of north latitude

strikes the River Iroquois or Cataraqui thence along the middle of said river into Lake Ontario, through the middle of said Lake until it strikes the communication by water between that Lake and Lake Erie; thence along the middle of said communication into Lake Erie; through the middle of said Lake until it rises at the water communication between that Lake and Lake Huron; thence along the middle of said water communication into the middle of Lake Huron; thence through the middle of said Lake to the water communication between that Lake and Lake Superior; thence through Lake Superior, Northward of the Isles Royal and Phelipeaux, to the Long Lake; thence through the middle of said Long Lake, and the water communication between it and the Lake of the Woods, to the said Lake of the Woods; thence through the said Lake to the most North-Western point thereof, and from thence in a due West course to the River Mississippi.

From the St Lawrence river up to Lake Superior each side has fared reasonably well, Canada, for example, having secured Wolfe Island which dominates the City of Kingston, and the United States having got some advantage in other islands. A sensible arrangement was come to whereby all the channels and passages in the rivers St Lawrence, Detroit and St Clair should be equally free to the traffic of both countries, as also all communications between Lake Superior and the Lake of the Woods.

Much more important was the determination of the boundary from "Long Lake" in Lake Superior to the Pacific ocean. To understand the insistence with which the American claim was urged it is necessary to recall some of the history of the United States. As far back as the 17th century France and the English Adventurers of the Hudson's Bay Company had been rivals for the North-West fur-trade. At first this was confined to the neighbourhood of the Hudson's Bay, the West being still unexplored. South of them lay Quebec which stretched as far as the Mississippi. Down this river the French explorer La Salle had gone and in 1682 took possession of the whole basin under the authority of France, and gave it the name "Louisiana" in honour of Louis XIV. Of the country west of this and of the region beyond the sources of the Mississippi hardly anything was known. After the treaty of Utrecht the English always claimed that the boundary between Hudson's Bay and Quebec ran from a point on the Labrador Coast to the present Lake Abitibi, at latitude 49°, and from this point due west indefinitely. The line was placed on most maps though never formally sanctioned by any commissioners, and the English maintained that the French had no rights north of it[1].

With the cession of Quebec in the treaty of 1763 the whole situation changed. Great Britain claimed that Canada extended to the Wabash, thence down the Wabash to its confluence with the Ohio, thence down the Ohio to the Mississippi, thence up the Mississippi to its source. Only Louisiana west of the Mississippi was left to the French, but for the Americans the important fact was that in 1774, by Imperial Act, Quebec was extended west to the Mississippi and was made to include what is now part of Minnesota, Wisconsin, Illinois, Indiana, Michigan and Ohio. In effect a barrier was placed against what they regarded as their legitimate western expansion, by which they were so angered that it became one of the counts in their grievances against Britain.

The next step was taken in the treaty of 1783. In the negotiations of 1782 leading up to this treaty the Americans attempted to get the line of the 45th degree from the St Lawrence to the Mississippi, but the British would not give up the Great Lakes and the large fertile area which now constitutes the best portion of Ontario. So we have the compromise of the line of the St Lawrence through the Lakes to the Lake of the Woods. But where was the "Long Lake" of Article II of the treaty, emptying into Lake Su-

[1] *Canadian Historical Review*, vol. IV, p. 129.

perior and connecting with the Lake of the Woods?
It existed only on Mitchell's map. According to
David Thompson the explorer, than whom none
knew the country better, the main fur-trade route
from the Lake of the Woods to Lake Superior
followed the river St Louis, at the mouth of which
Duluth now stands, and this river is probably what
Mitchell meant by "Long Lake." Therefore, had not
both maps and knowledge been defective, and had
the treaty been carried out according to the historical
conditions of the trade, as seems to have been its
intent, the Canadian boundary would to-day run
from Duluth up the St Louis River to the Lake of the
Woods, making a large addition of most valuable
land to the Dominion. But by a compromise Ashburton and Webster in 1842 chose the Pigeon River
on Lake Superior to denote the imaginary "Long
Lake" of the treaty. At this point another correction
in the treaty was made owing to the discovery that a
line drawn due west from the north-western point of
the Lake of the Woods does not strike the Mississippi
river. At that time it was supposed that the source
of the Mississippi was north of the Lake of the
Woods, and it was not until 1797 that it was discovered to be south.

The movement of the American was towards the
West. A vision of his future is embodied in the North
West Ordinance of 1787 by which "the wide vacant

territory west of the (Allegheny) mountains was declared a national domain, a reserve tract out of which,
as the population increased, new states should be
created with rights equal in every way to those of the
old ones[1]." This Ordinance was one of the most
important decisions in the early history of the United
States, and is quite intelligible to the Canadian who
remembers what the acquisition of the North-West
meant for Canada. Jefferson read well the rising
national consciousness when he boldly concluded the
"Louisiana Purchase" with France in 1803. This
gave the United States at a comparatively small cost
the immense territory since delimited into the states
of western Louisiana, Arkansas, Wisconsin, Iowa,
western Minnesota, the Dakotas, Nebraska, Kansas
and parts of Montana, Wyoming, Colorado and
Oklahoma. Once this purchase was effected it became necessary to determine the boundary, which
according to letters-patent given to the original
grantee did not lie beyond the area drained by the
western tributaries to the Mississippi, and certainly
did not reach as far north as the 49th parallel. But
little was known of the whole region, and it was a
natural procedure to extend the line to the 49th
parallel which had been the former demarcation
between Hudson's Bay territory and New France.

[1] A. C. Coolidge, *The United States as a World Power*,
p. 28.

Thus in 1818 this became the accepted boundary between the two countries as far as the Rocky mountains.

For a decade the further extension of the boundary beyond the Rockies was not seriously discussed, but much was happening that was bound in time to produce trouble. The Americans pushed on to the West without ceasing; their dream of reaching the Pacific by land had never faded. As far back as 1791 M. de Warville wrote in his *Travels in North America*:

In September 1790 the Ship *Columbia*, Captain Gray, sailed to discover the North-West of this continent: this is his second voyage round the world: the Brig *Hope* has sailed for the same object. Our papers have resounded with the quarrels of the English and Spaniards for the commerce of Nootka Sound. The Americans make no quarrels: but they have already made a considerable commerce on the same coast in furs and peltry. They were there trading in the year 1789 in good intelligence with both parties. In the same year no less than forty-four vessels were sent from the single town of Boston to the North-West of America, to India and to China. They bound not their hopes there; they expect some day to open a communication more direct to Nootka Sound. It is probable that this place is not far from the headwater of the Mississippi; which the Americans will soon navigate to its source, when they shall begin to people Louisiana and the interior of New Mexico[1].

To Thomas Jefferson's foresight was due not only the "Louisiana Purchase" in 1803, but the com-

[1] Quoted in *A Century of Population*, p. 29.

missioning of Lewis and Clark to find some access by water to the Pacific. They were the first to traverse the waters of the Columbia down to the sea, which they reached in 1805. All this time, however, there were shrewd and enterprising men on the North, chiefly servants of the North-West Company, who were making a parallel race for the western ocean, but these men had no plans for colonisation: they sought only to conserve the fur-trade for their masters. In July 1793, Alexander MacKenzie, after crossing the mountains from the east, was the first white man to see the Pacific from that direction; in 1800, Duncan McGillivray, a fur trader, was the first to reach the upper waters of the Columbia. In the next few years the North-West Company sought to extend its trade beyond the Rockies as quickly as possible lest it should be forestalled by its rival, the Hudson's Bay Company. In 1806, Simon Fraser had established trading posts on the Fraser river, the first settlement made by white men in this "Oregon" region. Thompson established Fort Kootenae on the Upper Columbia in 1807, and by 1810 four posts had been built south of the 49th parallel. The rivalry between the two companies was brought to an end in 1821 by the absorption, not without much discontent, of the North-West Company in that of the Hudson's Bay, which thus became for more than twenty years the dominating power throughout the vast territories of what is now British Columbia and a part of Oregon.

But there is another side to the story, the approach from the Pacific. For two centuries and a half the Spaniards had been visiting these shores, the whole of which they claimed on the strength of settlements made on the southern portion only. Their jurisdiction was challenged from time to time by such English sailors as Drake, Cook and Vancouver, who, unlike the Spaniards, built up a considerable trade. Trouble broke out between them in Nootka Sound on Vancouver Island in 1790, shortly after which it was agreed by treaty that "neither the one nor the other of the two parties shall make any permanent establishment in the said port, or claim there any right of sovereignty or territorial dominion to the exclusion of the other. And their said Majesties will assist each other mutually to maintain to their subjects free access to the said port of Nootka against any other nation which should attempt to establish there any sovereignty or dominion;" but Britain always held that by reason of her settlement and trade her claims were superior to those of Spain. In February 1819 the United States acquired by treaty with Spain all her rights on the Pacific north of the 42nd degree of latitude, and thus became the leading power on the coast.

In the North the Russians were in control. As far

back as 1741 they got a foothold in Alaska under the leadership of Behring, a Dane. Eighty years afterwards the Czar arrogantly forbade "all foreign vessels not only to land on the coasts and islands between Behring Strait and the 51st parallel ...... but also to approach them within less than a hundred Italian miles" under penalty of confiscation of vessel and cargo. Both Britain and the United States protested strongly, and a treaty was concluded making Russia's southern boundary 54° 40'.

In 1792 Gray, the American already referred to, entered the Columbia river, but it was a lieutenant of Vancouver's who shortly afterwards explored it for 100 miles and formally took possession of it in the name of Great Britain. In 1811 an American fur company established a fort at the mouth of the river, called Astoria, after its founder, John Jacob Astor. On the outbreak of war in 1812 it was sold to the North-West Company in order to prevent capture, but was restored on the declaration of peace. The purpose of the Americans never slumbered. It was expressed in the words of Adams to Rush, the Minister to England, in 1818:

If the United States leave her [Britain] in undisturbed enjoyment of all her holds upon Europe, Asia and Africa, with all her actual possessions in this hemisphere, we may very fairly expect that she will not think it consistent either with a wise or a friendly policy to watch with eyes of jealousy and alarm every possibility of extension to our own natural dominion in North America, which she can have no solid interest to prevent.

So this magnificent prize lay under the jealous eyes of the two watchers, the one, however, more alert than the other. By a convention in 1818 and again in 1827 the territory west of the Rockies was left free for joint occupancy by settlers and traders from Britain or the United States.

After 1821 the Hudson's Bay Company entered on a new phase of its career and it was well served by its officials, of whom one of the greatest was Dr John McLaughlin, chief factor in this region for many years. In 1824–5 he built Fort Vancouver on the Columbia river six miles above its junction with the Willamette, "like a medieval castle, at once a refuge in time of danger, an oasis of civilization in a surrounding desert of barbarism, and a capital from which its commander ruled the adjacent territory[1]." This occupancy of the disputed country and the success of the Company aroused the sleepless policy of the Americans, and the frontiersman began to appear in Oregon, followed in 1834 by missionaries, whose patriotism in winning Oregon for the United States was at least equal to their zeal in carrying the Gospel to the Indian and the new settler. They came

[1] Coats and Gosnell, *Sir James Douglas*, p. 110.

as a crusade: "Every settler was a soldier and his wife and family part of an American garrison[1]." But they were faced by famine and other dangers which would have obliterated them had not McLaughlin come to their rescue; very unwisely he even helped them to form a provisional government, but they requited him with ingratitude, and on account of his kindness to them he lost his place with the Hudson's Bay Company. By 1845 the stream of immigration had broadened out over the country, Americans to the number of 6,000 made their homes in the new territory, and thus by actual possession they established for the United States a strong argument for its ownership.

But American opinion had not been unanimous as to extending the jurisdiction of the United States beyond the Rockies. Even Webster and Gallatin would have preferred a friendly Pacific republic[2]. But not so the rank and file. Under Polk's electioneering cry in 1844 of "Fifty-four forty or fight" the masses were worked up to such a pitch that when he became President he found that he had raised a very difficult issue, for England responded with ominous mutterings, and she refused to listen to suggestions for negotiation. Even the Canada of those days, far distant and small, was stirred, as represented by the Toronto *Globe*:

[1] *Op. cit.* p. 156.   [2] Foster, *op. cit.* pp. 309–13.

Great Britain has for many years treated the United States government unlike any other.... But there must be bounds to such forbearance, for it only brings fresh insult and injury in return. War is a frightful evil, but it is often necessary to teach a lesson of wisdom to the world, and never did a nation require it more than the United States.

"Had England," wrote Bancroft, "been as unreasonable, overbearing and insulting as the people of the United States, there assuredly would have been war[1]," and even the Hon. J. W. Foster admits that their claims were not beyond dispute. But better counsels prevailed on both sides; negotiations were entered into in 1846, the decision of which was that the boundary should follow the 49th parallel from the Rockies to "the middle of the channel which separates the continent from Vancouver's Island; and thence southerly through the middle of the said channel and of Fuca's Strait to the Pacific Ocean." The Columbia river was to be freely navigable by the servants of the Hudson's Bay Company whose lands in this territory might be purchased by the United States at a proper valuation. Some years later when the Company found the new regime irksome and their future likely to be precarious, they sold their rights to the United States for six hundred and fifty thousand dollars, and they left the country in 1869. Thereafter, Victoria, now the beautiful capital of

[1] *Canada and its Provinces*, VIII, p. 869 *n.*

British Columbia, founded by Sir James Douglas in 1843, came into great importance. By this treaty, Britain got the whole of the magnificent Vancouver Island which runs south nearly to the 48th parallel.

It was fortunate that the dispute was settled in 1846, for ten years later gold was discovered in the valley of the Fraser river, and a very large number of the inrushing miners were Americans. Had they urged the claim of occupation as they did in Oregon, Britain might have come off even worse than she did in the Treaty of 1846.

The Canadian as he turns out of Victoria harbour on his way to Vancouver finds to his surprise opposite him, distant only some six or seven miles and almost blocking his way, the large island of St Juan, succeeded further north by smaller ones, on which the American flag flies. On St Juan there was in the late sixties almost a clash of arms, and the dispute as to ownership was referred for solution to the German Emperor in 1871. He had to decide what was meant in the treaty of 1846 by "the channel which separates the continent from Vancouver's Island." He gave a decision in favour of the Americans, and the Haro Strait, the furthest west of the three channels, became the boundary.

A review of the negotiations from 1783 to 1871 leads to the conclusion that in consideration of the knowledge of the country and of the reasonable expectations of its future, Britain not only acted well on behalf of Canada, but pushed her claims with vigour and sagacity. In respect of the far West it must be remembered that, as the late Christopher Robinson said at the time of the Commission on the Alaskan Boundary, "until the completion of the Canadian Pacific Railway, Canada knew more of Egypt than she did of British Columbia." But credit must also be given to the Hudson's Bay and the North-West Companies for holding the Pacific province for Britain. Had it not been for them the United States might have been in possession of the whole coast to-day. Her negotiations were conducted without either indifference or ignorance. Her people had caught a vision of the far West as the Canadians did many years afterwards. They discerned by instinct that no rival must be allowed to bar their access to the Pacific. Spain had gone, France had gone, Russia was to go, and Britain alone seemed immovable; a Britain, moreover, which with each decade after the thirties was beginning to redress the loss of her revolted colonies by pouring her home-born population into the vacant spaces of Canada. It was no wonder if the Americans feared lest the vitality of the Empire, which they had thought to have driven from the best parts of the continent, might perchance revive and thwart them successfully in their ambitions for a powerful domain on the Pacific, and challenge their

F   5

supremacy in territory to which they felt they had at least an equal claim.

The Alaska Boundary, which was finally determined in the year 1903, occasioned the last of the great frontier disputes between the United States and Canada. Over twenty years have passed since the award was made, but though it is not much more than a memory Canadians still recall it as the one in which they were out-manœuvred in the process, whatever the judgment itself was. The problem had been awaiting decision for many years. It can be traced back even to the Russian treaty of 1825; it flared up at the time of the purchase of Alaska by the United States in 1867, and it was stirred again when British Columbia came into the Dominion in 1871. Frequent representations had been made in regard to it by the British Government, but the United States vouchsafed no response.

The Alaska Boundary question could have been settled without difficulty at any time for many years; there was no controversy about it, and it failed of settlement because our Congress was unwilling to make an appropriation to survey the boundary; and through that fatuous refusal to dispose of the question when there was no controversy, there came a most critical situation, the settlement of which was exceedingly difficult[1].

The issue became acute when gold was discovered in the Yukon in 1896. Miners, with such attendant

[1] Elihu Root, *Miscellaneous Addresses*, p. 154.

adventurers as seek fortunes or excitement where there is a rich strike poured into the territory, thronging the comparatively short but terrible trail that led from the port of Dyea or Skagway on the Lynn Canal. These ports of entry and egress the Americans claimed as theirs. Were they really so? This was the heart of the Alaska controversy. The ownership of the Portland Canal at the extreme south of Alaska was of minor importance. In 1898 the Canadian government endeavoured to get the Americans to come to a decision on the matter, and a commission was appointed of Canadian Ministers together with Lord Herschell on the one side, and American representatives on the other, to investigate (1) the Alaskan and Atlantic fisheries, (2) the Alaskan boundary, (3) trade relations, (4) limitation of warships on the Lakes, (5) bonding privileges and some minor matters. Progress was made in regard to questions in which the United States was especially interested, such as the Fisheries, but its representatives would not come to any agreement on the Alaskan boundary, nor make any concession whatever to the Canadians in the way of giving them an outlet. Lord Herschell, therefore, would not agree to any compromise on the Fisheries, much to the annoyance of John Hay, Secretary of State. Later, when the Americans wished to have the Clayton-Bulwer treaty abrogated, the Canadians demanded that their rights should be attended to, and

Hay was again annoyed. He referred to their claim as a "trumped-up charge," but Mr Root's remarks just quoted are sufficient to show that this was probably the petulant outburst of a wearied Secretary of State.

Upon this failure the British Commissioners asked for arbitration by a tribunal of jurists, based upon lines similar to those of the Venezuela settlement. But President Roosevelt, in strange disregard of the facts, gave expression to a widely held view that the Canadian claim was manufactured on account of the gold rush, and though his Ambassador to Britain counselled arbitration he refused to listen to him, distrusting his pro-English bias. Finally, in 1903 Mr Hay persuaded the Senate to consent to a treaty for the appointment of a tribunal of "six impartial jurists of repute" who were to consider judicially the questions submitted to them, "each of whom shall first subscribe an oath that he will impartially consider the arguments and evidence presented to the tribunal and will decide thereupon according to his true judgment." This was satisfactory, but when President Roosevelt appointed the Hon. Elihu Root, and Senators Lodge and Turner as the American "impartial jurists" a storm of dissent broke out in Canada and in Britain[1]. Mr Lodge had declared two

[1] Also the *Springfield Republican* in the United States criticized the selection.

years previously that "a more manufactured and baseless claim" had never been set up, and Senator Turner was politically committed to the interests of Seattle[1]. There seems to be no doubt that Roosevelt took the matter out of Hay's hands. In a letter to Justice Holmes, which he was told he might show "privately and unofficially" to Joseph Chamberlain, he wrote:

If there is a disagreement I wish it to be distinctly understood not only that there will be no arbitration of the matter, but that in my message to Congress I shall take a position which will prevent any possibility of arbitration hereafter... to run the line, as we claim it, by our own people without any further regard to the attitude of England and Canada[2].

The contemptuous tone of a part of the American press, the suggestion of another section of the press that the English representative would be won over, and injudicious remarks even of eminent men both

[1] It is interesting on the other hand to read in the recently published *Correspondence* between President Roosevelt and Henry Cabot Lodge that in the President's opinion Sir Wilfrid Laurier had shortly before set forth in a speech in Parliament at Ottawa "the claims which he apparently expects the Canadian members of the Tribunal to uphold as advocates rather than to consider as judges" (II, 4). A few months later he writes to Lodge: "We must not weaken on points of serious importance. It is unnecessary for me to say this for you all three feel it quite as strongly as I do" (II, 67).

[2] J. F. Rhodes, *The McKinley and Roosevelt Administrations*, p. 258. Cf. also *Roosevelt-Lodge Correspondence* (1925), II, 44 f.

east and west to the effect that the annexation of
Canada in the not distant future was "predetermined
and inevitable," heightened the tenseness of feeling
in the Dominion. From many Canadian quarters
came the demand that the British government should
refuse to take part in the tribunal, but the government of the Dominion appointed two representatives
and the Home government named the Chief Justice
of England, Lord Alverstone. Such was the preparation in both countries for this judicial Commission.

By the terms of the treaty the tribunal was to
decide: (1) Where the southern boundary began;
which is the Portland Channel; (2) Was it the intention and meaning of the Russian Convention of 1825
that there should remain in the exclusive possession
of Russia a continuous fringe of coast on the mainland not exceeding ten marine leagues in width separating the British possessions from the bays, ports,
inlets, havens and waters of the ocean from the 56th
degree of latitude north to the intersection of such
line with the 141st degree of latitude; (3) Should the
width of the fringe belonging to Russia be measured
from the general line of the mainland or from the
heads of the inlets, of which the most important was
the Lynn Canal on which Dyea and Skagway were
situated[1].

[1] See *Roosevelt-Lodge Correspondence* (1925), II, 5.

The only point on which unanimity was secured was that the southern boundary, the Portland channel, which had been surveyed and described by Vancouver in 1793, ran north of the two large islands Pearse and Wales. There agreement ended. The Americans held that the channel then ran between Wales and Sitklan, so that the latter and another small island belonged to the United States. With them Lord Alverstone agreed; but the two Canadians recorded violent dissent and asserted that their colleague had without warning to them changed his mind on this point in order to avoid a deadlock. Though this decision was of much less practical importance than the others, it occasioned deep feeling throughout Canada.

As in other boundary questions the chief remaining difficulties arose from the faulty maps that had been used for the original treaty. It had been assumed that there was a more or less continuous range of mountains parallel to the coast, but on actual survey this proved not to be so. It therefore became necessary to fall back upon the intent of the treaty. Sir Charles Bagot, who negotiated it, wrote: "It is evident to me that I cannot avoid giving some *lisière*, however narrow, upon the mainland[1]," because the Russians were bound to keep the British on the further side of the mountains in order to prevent the

[1] *Bagot Papers*, quoted in *Canada and its Provinces*, VIII, p. 952.

Hudson's Bay Company from getting any port from which it could trade upon the coast. This was taken by the Americans and Lord Alverstone to be the intent of the treaty, and in accordance therewith they decided that the crest of mountains about thirty miles from the general line of the coast should be the boundary, and that where there was no range near and parallel to the coast, the boundary should be at the east of a strip of land not exceeding ten leagues in width. The same judges ruled that the width of this strip should be measured from the heads of inlets or tide water. The effect of this decision was to exclude Canada from access to her Yukon trade through any port of her own upon the Pacific.

The announcement of the decision raised public opinion in Canada to a white heat. As expressed by a contemporary observer, the general conviction was that the decision was diplomatic, not judicial; that it was due to the British policy of cultivating friendship with the United States; but that the provocation, great though it was, would not seriously undermine loyalty to Great Britain[1]. Here and there men who had studied the question advised calmness, and some of those who were best acquainted with the Pacific coast openly stated that Canada's case was not as strong as had been popularly supposed. The Americans did little to alleviate the soreness of the Canadians. Some

[1] *Canadian Annual Review*, 1904, p. 374.

papers rather aggravated their temper with such words as "childish" or "churlish"; others again analyzed the outburst as indicating such discontent with Britain as would lead soon by natural destiny to annexation. But it was against the United States that Canada was really embittered, chiefly because President Roosevelt refused arbitration for the solution of the question. She could not forget President Cleveland's message to Britain in the Venezuelan case. The real root of bitterness lay in the origin and character of the commission, rather than in its foregone conclusion. Canada felt that her neighbour regarded her as a mere pawn in the imperial game. Even Sir Wilfrid Laurier was moved to say in Parliament: "I have often regretted, and never more than on the present occasion, that we are living beside a great neighbour, who I believe I can say without being unfriendly to them are very grasping in their national actions, and who are determined on every occasion to get the best in any agreement which they make. I have often regretted also that while they are a great and powerful nation, we are only a small colony, a growing colony, but still a colony." This was the utterance of Canadian disappointment with a touch of the politician's art, for at Ottawa it should have been known that Canada's position was not impregnable. It can hardly be maintained that the decision was due to imperial policy, and Canada alone could not have got better terms[1]. Whether the United States if she had desired to be a kindly neighbour might not have been somewhat generous in order to create better feelings in the Canadians is another matter. Trade may be a cause of neighbourliness or of irritation. But when commercial interests stir political passions generosity flies off in the storm.

Canadians and Americans both may be thankful that these boundary difficulties have been settled. Too often the final result was delayed until hostile activities created resentments and prejudices that have been far more injurious to both peoples than the loss of the territory in question would have been.

The International Joint Commission

After the outstanding disputes as to boundaries were settled there remained many lesser problems arising out of the long border which, while it separates the two countries, also serves to bring them together. Rivers and lakes occasion most of these difficulties. On the east there are the St John and the St Croix rivers; the Richelieu flows in quiet and full volume from lake Champlain across Quebec into

[1] Senator Lodge wrote to President Roosevelt: "The whole difficulty comes from the Canadians, and they [the English] are as timid about the Canadians as they can possibly be; they are so afraid of injuring their sensibilities that they hardly dare say anything." *Op. cit.* II, 42.

the St Lawrence; then come the St Lawrence and the Great Lakes as far as the Lake of the Woods; the Red river runs north from Dakota into Manitoba, the Souris further west; in Montana the St Mary and the Milk rivers take their rise, the former becoming tributary to the Saskatchewan, the latter after one hundred miles of tortuous flow returning to Montana to join the Missouri; and finally the Kootenay and the Columbia issuing from British Columbia find their course through Montana, Idaho, Washington and Oregon to the Pacific. These are waterways such as only a continent of vast spaces could feed, and they are also the heart and arterial system of the most important half of North America. The life of both peoples depends upon them.

It is hard for those who have not sailed on the Great Lakes to realise their magnitude. They constitute one of the chief highways of the world. Large passenger steamers traverse the distance from Duluth or Fort William to Buffalo in fifty hours, through Lakes Superior, Huron and Erie, past Sault Ste Marie, Sarnia, Detroit and Cleveland; it is said that including the traffic to and from Chicago and on Lake Ontario, not less than fifteen million persons travel on these waters in one season. In the autumn fleets of carriers filled with grain pass up and down the same route and other ships laden with cargoes of great variety come and go in all directions. Probably not less than one hundred million tons of freight are carried annually, and the tonnage on the Detroit river, though it is open to navigation only for eight months, is more than three times that on the Suez Canal during the entire year.

These Lakes are bordered by some of the richest and most thickly settled sections of the United States and Canada. Here the lives of the two peoples blend in fullest volume. The cities on their shores get their water supply from them, and into them also they drain their sewage; they turn to them for water-power as well as for transport. Moreover, what one remote locality does may influence millions of people who live a thousand miles away. The erection of a dam far up in the Lake of the Woods affected an area of 26,000 square miles, capital of one hundred million dollars invested in it, and the welfare of cities so far apart as Winnipeg and Duluth. Recently the city of Chicago, at the foot of Lake Michigan, has been diverting a large quantity of the water of the lake into the Chicago river for the disposal, so it has been asserted, of its sewage, but cities on the other lakes, both American and Canadian, have entered a complaint because this diversion has lowered the channels of navigation and may reduce the quantity of available hydro-electric power at Niagara.

Almost as important is the demand, insistent and increasing from the western states and the north-west

provinces of Canada, that the canals on these waterways shall be deepened in order that sea-going
vessels may carry grain and other products from the
head of the Great Lakes to Europe.

It is obvious how vast are the issues involved in the
joint possession of these lakes and rivers, and how
delicately interwoven they are between the two
countries. Canada is mistress of the Welland canal
that unites lakes Erie and Ontario, and of the gateway to the ocean on the St Lawrence. The question
is no longer as to where an invisible line runs, but as
to how such an equitable joint use and development
may be made of these waterways and powers that the
health, intercourse, trade and general well-being of
both peoples may be promoted. Many occasions of
friction have arisen on this tide of commerce, but
there are no defensive warships on these waters, no
arsenals on the shores, and except for customs regulations the traffic flows as it would between two sections
of one people.

A different importance attaches to the rivers on
the prairies which cross the international boundary.
In the far West where the dry belt runs through
Montana and enters southern Alberta, the rivers are
the chief, often indeed the only, source for irrigation.
The construction of a dam or a canal in one country
which would cut off the supply of water in the other,
might therefore almost ruin the homes of thousands

of their neighbours, and bring on a crisis which would be quite as dangerous to international goodwill as were the undetermined boundaries.

To solve the numerous and varied problems such as arose from the situation that has been outlined, the United States and Canada have created an International Joint Commission. They have been fortunate indeed in this original undertaking, and it is a matter for surprise that a commission as unique as it has been successful in its procedure has attracted so little attention either at home or abroad. To understand its formation it is necessary to go back to 1902, when by concurrent legislation the two governments created the International Waterways Commission, of six members, whose duties were simply to investigate and report on the conditions and uses of the waters of the Lakes, the maintenance and regulation of levels and the effect of diversions of the flow upon structures on the banks or in the streams. That Commission did good work, but Mr Root wished to go further: "(His) desire was to dispense with the Hague tribunal as far as concerns matters between the United States and Canada, and set an example to the world by the creation of a judicial board as distinguished from a diplomatic and partizan agency[1]." This purpose took shape in a treaty which was brought about

[1] See articles by Mr L. J. Burpee, Canadian Secretary of the Joint Commission.

by the joint efforts of the two statesmen, Mr Root, then Secretary of State, and Mr James Bryce, at that time Ambassador Extraordinary at Washington. By this treaty a commission or court was to be created to which large powers were to be assigned for dealing with matters pertaining to both countries. The Senate of the United States ratified it in 1909; the Parliament of Canada confirmed it in 1911, and the first meeting of the Commission for organization was held at Washington in January 1912. The Commission consisted of six members, three appointed by the President of the United States and three by the King on the recommendation of the Governor-General-in-Council of Canada.

Its purpose was two-fold: to settle questions that were pending along the common frontier, and to prevent, if possible, or to make provision for the adjustment and settlement of similar difficulties in the future, even such as might not be frontier questions. So important are several articles of the treaty that further brief attention may be given to them.

In the first article it was agreed that the navigation of all boundary waters shall be for ever free and open to both countries equally, and that during the life of the treaty the same rights shall extend to the waters of Lake Michigan and to all canals connecting boundary waters, and that the rules, regulations and tolls on these canals shall apply alike to the people of both countries.

By the second article

any interference with or diversions from their natural channel of such waters on either side of the boundary resulting in any injury to the other side of the boundary, shall give rise to the same rights and entitle the injured parties to the same legal remedies as if such injury took place in the country where such diversion or interference occurs.

This article means that a Canadian may have recourse to American courts for redress if he believes that any interference with the flow of water on the American side has done him any injury. Similarly, the American may appeal to Canadian courts. The range of this article is extraordinary: "Its effect is to erase the boundary and pool the resources of American and Canadian courts for the benefit of the people on both sides of these waterways."

The third article provides that in the future any obstruction or diversion of waters on either side that affects the levels or flow of boundary waters shall not be permitted without the consent of the Commission; and the fourth article also prohibits pollution that may do injury to health or property. There is an order of precedence for the uses of the water: (1) for domestic and sanitary purposes, (2) for navigation, (3) for power and irrigation.

The ninth article provides that any other questions

or matters of difference involving rights, obligations or interests along the common frontier shall be referred to the Commission for examination and report if either government shall request such a reference. Their recommendations, however, are not to be regarded as decisions, nor as having the character of an arbitral award.

But the tenth article has even greater potential importance. The Senate of the United States and His Majesty's Government, with the consent of the Governor-General-in-Council, may by joint consent refer to the Commission any question or matter of difference that may arise between them or the inhabitants of the two countries. In this case a majority of the Commission may render a decision or finding on the question referred to it. If unable to render such a decision they shall report to their governments, and the question shall thereupon be referred by the two governments to an umpire chosen according to the procedure of the Hague Convention of 1907, and his decision shall be final. This article gives the Commission remarkable powers. Any question, apparently, may be referred to it, not merely such matters of dispute as may arise on the frontier. But it is probable that no government would hand over to such a tribunal questions of acute national policy, though the *American Journal of International Law* expressed this opinion in 1912: "It is not too much to say that (it) constitutes a permanent international tribunal between Canada and the United States to which any questions or matters arising between them may be referred and decided by the principles of law and justice." In fact, the Commission has been described by an eminent Canadian Judge as "a miniature Hague Tribunal for the United States and Canada."

The members of the Commission do not speak or vote as representing their national point-of-view, but with the realization that they are expected to promote the interests which the people hold in common; and so successfully has the tribunal hitherto fulfilled its purpose that no suggestion has been made to terminate the treaty, though since 1915 this might have been done by either party giving twelve months' written notice to the other. During its existence some twenty-five decisions have been made, and it is a fine testimony both to the gentlemen who have composed the tribunal and to the goodwill of both peoples that all these decisions have been unanimous.

In this procedure surely we have a pledge and an earnest of a permanent and better way of dealing between these two nations than theretofore existed. But if the Commission is to realize its possibilities its work must become better known. Intelligent Americans and Canadians should be made aware that this splendid instrument which has been used so effectively lies ready to hand. If it were to appeal to the imagination with something of the dignity and prestige of a great court, the members having the status of judges, independent and unaffected by party affiliations, the Commission might in time have wider questions referred to it than any that have yet been brought before it. These judges could not be allowed to become the umpires of national policies. Neither people would consent to take these from their legislatures and hand them to a court, however distinguished. But many matters might be dealt with before they reach the stage of national policy, which if taken early need not develop into international issues. Experience and wisdom speaking from a tribunal which has popular respect might solve these without raising the dust of controversy.

The project of the development of the St Lawrence waterway for ocean-going shipping and for the creation of electric power from the canalization works involved has been before the people of both countries for many years. Consideration was suspended during the War, but in 1919 Congress expressed a desire that the International Joint Commission should investigate the problem of its feasibility and cost. The Commission reported in 1922, and in the same year the American government communicated in regard to it with the Canadian government, which took action in 1924. The United States was ready to negotiate a treaty but Canada hesitated on account of the cost and the magnitude of the questions involved. However, a committee of engineers from both nations is at work investigating the formulation of the problems which are to be considered by both countries. If this project is carried out it will probably be more significant for Canada than for the United States, as she holds the strategic position; but a mutually satisfactory solution would bind the two countries in closer friendly relations.

CHAPTER III

Fisheries Disputes

THE ATLANTIC FISHERIES

THE recurrent controversies occasioned by the taking of fish in territorial waters or the open sea have periodically aroused deep resentment against the United States because the people of the provinces believed that the action of the Americans was an invasion of their natural rights, to say nothing of the interference with their already sufficiently precarious means of livelihood. All around the coasts of Nova Scotia and New Brunswick the bays and harbours are dotted with fishermen's houses, and though in some parts these folk have thriven, their living is subject to great fluctuations. They are first-class sailors and have built for themselves a fleet of staunch vessels in which they ply their fishing on the Grand Banks during the spring and summer; they also fish in the bays and along the shores. The bank fishing consists chiefly of cod; the in-shore of mackerel, herring, haddock, lobster and swordfish.

Their great rivals sail from Gloucester, Massachusetts, as their predecessors have done for many generations. More than a century and a half ago some of these New England people placed their homes on the southern shores of Nova Scotia, and their descendants still bear names that prove their affinity with families on Cape Cod and its vicinity. But during the nineteenth and twentieth centuries the movement has all been in the other direction. A large proportion of the crews of the Gloucester fleet are "blue-noses[1]," and it was no mere chance that in the international race of deep-sea fishing vessels in 1923 the captain of the Gloucester competitor was a Nova Scotian by birth. The life aboard these trim Gloucester schooners has been depicted in *Captains Courageous*; and their trade was thus described by Mr Root in his argument before the North Atlantic Fisheries Arbitrators:

The ships leave the Massachusetts and the Maine coasts at the very end of the winter, the beginning of spring, the last of February or the first of March, and they go up to the Banks, take as many fish as they can with the bait that they can carry and keep, and then they go to the nearest point to get bait and back to the Banks...they go to and fro for bait. Even if bait were unlimited down on the Massachusetts coast, the long voyage for a sailing vessel to get it and back again would exhaust the time which they should expend in catching cod-fish. The Bank season ends along in the autumn, and the vessels which are employed in it must either lie up and the men employed in it sit idle until the next spring, or some other occupation must be found. This winter herring fishery affords occupation for vessels and men during the off-season of the Bank-fishery, and so enables that fishery to be prosecuted profitably.

[1] The origin of this name for people of the Maritime provinces, and more especially Nova Scotia, is uncertain.

Though these Gloucester fishermen have natural disadvantages as compared with their rivals, they have the more than compensating immense market of the United States close at hand. This has been usually shut against the Canadians who therefore have to sell much of their catch in Europe and in the West Indies. But the Americans could not conduct profitable fishing on the Grand Banks if they were not allowed to get wood and water and harbour protection in distress; they would be seriously handicapped if they were refused ice and bait at the nearest ports, and inconvenienced if they could not ship their fresh catch through Maritime ports to the United States. Clearly it was a case for bargaining if the Canadians had absolute rights within their own territorial waters. This, however leads us back to the Treaty of 1783.

The third article was one of those most strongly debated. The colonial Americans knew well the value of the fisheries, as being one of their chief sources of food supply, and claimed that they had developed them, though in fact they had entered into a heritage which through centuries had belonged in succession to Bretons, Spanish, French and English. But they were successful in wresting from England in her weakness the concession of continuing to enjoy unmolested the "right" to all the advantages which the inhabitants of British North America and Newfoundland had as to fishing, and to dry their fish on any unsettled bays, harbours or creeks of Nova Scotia, the Magdalene Islands and Labrador. This was from the beginning a source of trouble. New settlers on the southern shores of Nova Scotia found fishing more profitable than farming, but everywhere they met their more experienced rivals from New England. Britain made great efforts to have these liberties of the Americans cancelled at the conclusion of the War in 1814, but to no purpose. Their argument was that these fishing rights were permanent and could not be alienated by the result of the War any more than their independence. In the years that followed there was much friction. Britain, however, grew in strength, and asserted her power in proportion, securing in the Convention of 1818 radical changes from the Treaty of 1783. She required that the United States should renounce for ever the liberty which she had hitherto claimed of fishing within the three-mile limit and of taking fish in-shore, except on the Magdalene Islands and on a section of the Labrador and the New-foundland coast; and of drying or curing fish except on unsettled bays, harbours and creeks of the southern coast of Newfoundland and the coast of Labrador.

Mr Root tells the story of the American reaction to this treaty:

When the War of 1812 was ended, a war waged over the question of impressments and not affecting the fisheries or involving as a matter of controversy the fisheries in any degree—when that War was ended without settling the question of impressments, without any particular credit to either side, the people of New England awoke to the startling and shocking realisation of the fact that their fisheries, their great industry, was gone, provided Great Britain could maintain that position, unanticipated, unexpected and a cause for chagrin. That is the explanation of the vehemence of John Quincy Adams in conducting the controversy and the meaning of his deep feeling and indignation. The proposition of Great Britain that the grant of this right was not permanent was a blow at the vital interest of the New England sea-board, and an absolute pre-requisite and *sine qua non* of the settlement of that controversy on the part of the United States was that, while she was forced to give up, while under this argument of Lord Bathurst she was out faced, borne down and compelled to give up the greater part of the rights she had held under the Treaty of 1783, the little remnant that she saved was to be made permanent beyond any possibility of doubt. That is a dominant feature in the article of the Treaty of 1818[1].

Smouldering trouble broke out in 1836 when Nova Scotia passed a "Hovering Act" to legalise the seizure of foreign vessels hovering within three miles of her coasts and harbours. But the New Englanders took the risks, and "in 1851 over one hundred vessels were driven ashore on Prince Edward Island in a gale and over three hundred lives were lost. The fleet braved the storm rather than run for port and thus confess their infraction of the British rights[2]." In

[1] *North Atlantic Fisheries Arbitration*, pp. 47 f.
[2] C. C. Tansill, *The Canadian Reciprocity Treaty of* 1854 (1922), p. 40.

the following year a British fleet was stationed in the Maritime waters and in reply President Fillimore sent a commodore to protect American fishermen. The Senate virtually said "England can have war if she wants it," and Daniel Webster expressed his countrymen's feeling when he asked, "What right have those distant and petty Provinces to deprive our fishermen of privileges which they have enjoyed since 1818, to seize our vessels and adjudicate their rights in their municipal tribunals?"

A change had taken place in the fishing. Mackerel and herring had come to be more important than cod, and as they had to be pursued in-shore the Americans came as far as they could into the open bays. This led to a controversy as to the meaning of the term "bay" in the Convention of 1818 which was not settled for many years. Meantime Britain made friendly overtures to the United States, though the people of the Maritime provinces then, as later, resented an attitude of concession, and in 1854 the matter was put to rest for twelve years by the passing of the Reciprocity treaty, whereby in return for reciprocal free-trade between the two countries the Americans were allowed the same privileges as the people of the Maritime provinces in fishing, curing the catch and the use of harbours.

On the abrogation of the treaty in 1866 the old troubles reappeared, and so seriously that the question was submitted to a Joint High Commission at Washington in 1871, together with the *Alabama* claims which at that time the British were especially anxious to have settled. The other representatives were often irritated at the interjection of the Fisheries dispute, but Sir John Macdonald, a most reluctant but independent commissioner, stood firm against British impatience and American petulance. Canada was still smarting from the injuries of the Fenian Raids, consideration of which the Americans ruled out while Britain was intent on negotiating the *Alabama* demands. To Macdonald the Americans were blustering neighbours: "they want everything and will give us nothing in exchange." After protracted discussion the United States offered fish and fish-oil free entry in return for the in-shore fisheries except in the mouths of rivers, and agreed to arbitrate the money equivalent for the difference in values. The Commission appointed for this purpose, presided over by a Belgian, met in Halifax in 1877 and decided that the United States should pay $5,500,000 as excess value of the fisheries for twelve years[1]. Congress was persuaded with some difficulty by President Hayes to pay it, and in this case Canada fared remarkably well.

The scene changed to Newfoundland in 1878 when American fishermen were attacked by a mob in Fortune Bay on the ground that they were using nets

[1] J. B. Moore, *Digest of American Treaties*, p. 753.

that injured the fisheries and that they were working on Sunday. The Government disowned the action of the mob and paid damages, but the incident brought the dispute into a new phase: first, how far were local regulations of Newfoundland binding upon Americans, and, secondly, what constitutes in-shore fishery? or, in other words, what is a "bay"? These questions were of great importance to Canada also, but they were not finally answered until the Hague Commission gave judgment in 1910.

The treaty of 1871 was abrogated in 1885 and automatically the Convention of 1818 came into force, but the Americans continued to infringe the regulations. They complained of "medieval restrictions on free navigation" and "Canadian inhumanity," and asserted that in 1886–7 over two thousand of their vessels were boarded or seized. Congress threatened retaliation. Another important international commission, appointed in 1888, recommended concessions to the Americans, but the Senate on a strict party vote threw out the treaty in order to discredit Cleveland[1]. A temporary *modus vivendi* was, however, arranged for a period not exceeding two years, and this continued in force from year to year until January 1924. By this American fishing vessels were permitted on payment of a nominal license fee to fish around the Magdalene Islands and on a portion of the

[1] R. M. McElroy, *Grover Cleveland*, I, pp. 295 f.

north shore of the Gulf of St Lawrence, to enter all bays and harbours on the Canadian coast, to purchase bait, ice, seines, lines or outfit, to transfer catches and to ship crews. But they were forbidden to fish or prepare to fish in territorial waters.

Newfoundland again became such a potential centre for dangerous storms that Mr Root and Mr Bryce induced their governments in 1908 to have articles framed embodying questions covering the points in dispute which should be referred to the Hague Tribunal. The award, made in 1910, was favourable to Britain. Among the decisions of present interest only two need be mentioned. The contention was upheld that Great Britain had sovereignty to make rules and regulations as to the conduct of her own people and on her own domain without securing the consent of the United States, but "such regulations must be *bona fide* and not in violation of the treaty of 1818—reasonable, as being, for instance, appropriate or necessary for the protection and preservation of such fisheries; desirable on grounds of public order and morals; equitable and fair as between local fishermen and the inhabitants of the United States"; and the Court of the Hague was made in all matters the final court of appeal.

The second decision was of greater importance for Canada: What is a "bay," or how is the line to be determined from which in large indentations on the shores the three-mile limit is to be measured? This award was in favour of Canada. Following the recommendation of the unratified Chamberlain-Bayard treaty of 1888, the bays that belong to Canada and Newfoundland were named, and within the larger expanses, such as Chaleur Bay, a limit was definitely fixed, so that fishermen in these areas might know when they were upon the high seas. All other bays were to have a line drawn across them from headland to headland where they are ten miles wide, from which the three-mile limit was to be measured; after a width of ten miles the indentation "ceases to have the configuration and characteristics of a bay." On the coasts of Delaware and Chesapeake Bays, however, this limit does not apply.

Both parties professed to be satisfied with the award, but almost equally important with the decision was the creation of the precedent of referring disputes to the Hague Court. Mr Root quotes with satisfaction these words from the judgment:

It furnishes an example of the peaceful and harmonious settlement of international disputes which will not, it is to be hoped, be without influence upon the world at large when it feels and responds, as in the course of time it must, to the pressure of an irresistible, and enlightened, public opinion in favour of the judicial settlement of justiciable disputes[1].

In a former chapter the work of this broad-minded

[1] Root, *op. cit.* XLVIII.

statesman in co-operating with Mr Bryce in the creation of the International Joint Commission has been referred to. It was a fortunate day for both countries when these two men were brought into diplomatic relationship.

For many years Canadians had heard little of the Atlantic Fisheries question. During the period from 1892 to 1923 efforts were made to secure for Canadian fishermen in return for the nominal license fee some advantages in United States ports, but to no purpose, except during the War when reciprocal privileges were granted; these, however, ceased in 1921, and in addition new tariff provisions of the Fordney Bill imposed further disabilities on the shipment of Canadian fish to the markets of the United States. Hence on December 31, 1923, the Canadian Government withdrew the *modus vivendi* which had been in effect since 1888, and thereafter American fishing vessels became subject again to the conditions of the Treaty of 1818, and can enter Canadian ports "only for shelter, for repairing damages, purchasing wood and obtaining water, and for no other purpose whatsoever." So the ancient problem is once more opened, though by the process of treaties and the changed conditions of the trade fishermen of the Maritime provinces have more and more become masters of their rich harvest of the sea.

THE FUR-SEAL ARBITRATION IN BEHRING SEA

The second great cognate dispute concerned the right of Canadians to take the fur-seal in Behring Sea. Historically this industry has none of the romance that attaches to the cod fisheries on the Banks of Newfoundland and in the Gulf of St Lawrence, and the killing of seals as a means of livelihood does not affect so many families as deep-sea fishing, nor is it pursued by the same class of men; but while the controversy lasted it was a long drawn out cause of irritation between the two countries.

Seal-fishing on the Pacific coast goes back to the last year of the eighteenth century when Paul I of Russia gave a charter to the Russian-American Company for carrying on hunting and trading "in the North-Eastern seas and along the coasts of America from the fifty-fifth degree of latitude to Behring Strait and also in the Aleutian, Kurile and other islands situated in the North-Eastern ocean." They were given the widest powers and exclusive advantages in respect of fishing, hunting and trading. By a ukase of 1821 the Emperor Alexander confirmed these privileges exclusively for Russian subjects as far as the fifty-first degree, and forbade all foreign vessels to approach within one hundred miles of the coast. This decree drew strong protests from both the British and the American governments, and after what they regarded as insufficient concessions on the part of Russia, they finally secured from her a convention signed by the latter in 1824, by the former a year later, according to which Russia agreed not to disturb or restrain the subjects of these negotiating powers in navigation, fishing or trading in these waters and with the natives of unoccupied districts.

During the Civil War in the United States Russia alone of European powers had favoured the North, and in 1867–8 disposed of Alaska to Washington for $7,200,000, hoping in making the transfer to help to expel Britain from the Pacific coast. The Government of the United States then made it unlawful for any person "to kill any otter, mink, marten, sable, or fur-seal, or other fur-bearing animal within the limits of the said territory or in the waters thereof," but the first indication of serious action on their part was given in 1881 in a letter from the Secretary of the Treasury, stating that all waters within the boundary of the Russian line from the Behring Strait leading south-west "to the western end of the Aleutian Archipelago and the chain of islands are considered as comprised within the waters of Alaska territory. All the penalties prescribed by law against the killing of fur-bearing animals would therefore attach against any violation of law within the limits before de-scribed."

The principle was first put into effect in 1886 by the seizure of three British Columbia sealers on the ground of their hunting and killing seals in the Alaskan preserves, though they were sixty miles from the Pribylov Islands. The captains and mates were fined and imprisoned, but on the strong protest of Britain they were released next year and no further action was taken. Meantime Canadian vessels were equipped and sent out, and several of them were seized and confiscated. In 1887 at the invitation of Mr Bayard the governments of France, Germany, Great Britain, Japan, Russia, Sweden and Norway agreed with the United States to take co-operative action for the protection of seals in the Behring Sea. But the Canadian government, to the great indignation of Mr Phelps, the American Ambassador in London, would not concur.

It is proposed (he wrote) by the colony of a foreign nation, in defiance of the joint remonstrance of all the countries interested, to destroy this business by the indiscriminate slaughter and extermination of the animals in question, in the open neighbouring sea, during the period of gestation when the common dictates of humanity ought to protect them were not interest at all involved.

Even Mr Phelps did not find it plain sailing in the uncharted and tortuous channels of the British Commonwealth.

Seizures of Canadian vessels began again in 1889,

and led to the passing of a bill in Congress which was really the assertion of "the doctrine of *mare clausum* in regard to a sea larger than the Mediterranean, and the gateway to which is four hundred and fifty miles wide," but the bill was so modified by the Senate that the regulations should "include and apply to all the dominion of the United States in the waters of Behring Sea." Though the claim to Behring Sea as a *mare clausum* was abandoned by Mr Blaine in his corespondence with Lord Salisbury in 1890, he took a new line of defence, maintaining that the pursuit of these seals by the Canadians was *contra bonos mores*, and in fact was piracy. Lord Salisbury replied to Mr Blaine that he was setting up a new theory of international law, that seals were *ferae naturae* and no man's property, and that the pursuit of them in the open sea had never been regarded as piracy in any civilized state. But he suggested that the matter should be referred to arbitration, and a treaty to this end was signed in 1892. Seven arbitrators were appointed—"jurists of distinguished reputation"— two British, two American, one named by the President of France, one by the King of Italy and one by the King of Norway and Sweden.

Five questions were submitted to the tribunal, of which the most important was, "Has the United States any, and if so what, right of protection or property in fur-seals frequenting the islands of the

United States in the Behring Sea when such seals are found outside the ordinary three-mile limit?" The cases were argued for the United States and Great Britain by Mr Root and Sir Charles Russell, respectively, the former with an ingenious and philosophical presentation, the latter with penetrating brilliancy and wit. In general the Americans argued that they were trustees of the herd for the benefit of mankind; Great Britain asserted the "freedom of the seas," and that no nation or individual had ever claimed property in a free swimming animal in the ocean. The United States argument, Russell said, came to this: "Put an end to pelagic sealing and we will recognize our duty as trustees to mankind by giving to mankind the benefit of the fur-seal at the market price."

By a majority the award went against the United States, and her claim was determined to have no foundation in history or in international law, but the tribunal, recognizing the precarious condition into which the industry had been brought, sought to effect by agreement what it could not grant by claim of right. It therefore drew up regulations which it recommended for adoption by the nations concerned forbidding their subjects to pursue the fur-seals within sixty miles of the Pribylov Islands, enjoining a closed season each year, requiring licenses for ships with definite equipment, and controlling as far as possible as regards fitness, the men who engage in it. These recommendations were adopted by both the British and United States governments.

The decision having been favourable to Britain, compensation was due to her for damages done through seizure of her vessels during the period of controversy, which was settled by arbitration at $425,000. But the United States still complained that the seals were being exterminated, especially by the Canadians, and negotiations dragged on intermittently and fruitlessly until 1911, when Great Britain on behalf of Canada entered into a conference at Washington with the United States, Russia and Japan for the protection of seals. A treaty concluded after the conference led to all the nations prohibiting pelagic seal-fishing for fifteen years, and Canada, which possessed no rookeries, was given a cash advance of $200,000 by the United States, to be repaid out of the annual percentage of the catch which would be Canada's share of the land catch of the other three nations. Canada did well financially; her share in the fishing was small and it was vanishing. By 1915 the herd of seals which had numbered two and a half millions in 1870–80 had been reduced to three hundred and forty thousand. The American rookeries are now owned by and are under the direction of the Secretary of Commerce at Washington, and in 1912 the Senate forbade land-killing of seals on the Pribylov Islands for five years, except such as are needed by the natives for food, the results of which combined measures are already seen in the increase of the herd.

The attitude of the American Government on the fur-seal business as compared with that on the Atlantic fisheries seems to a Canadian to have been shifted in accordance with the demands of sectional interests; and these were too small and ill-founded to have been worth the embroiling of the two nations in their settlement. But it would be hazardous for him to attempt to compare Vancouver with Seattle in respect of disinterestedness.

CHAPTER IV

Reactions on Canadian Nationalism

THE Constitution of the Dominion of Canada and the present national spirit of the people owe their character in part to the experience of the United States and to the propinquity of a powerful and often aggressive neighbour. Almost from the beginning the New England colonists looked upon the French in Canada as their natural enemies, and they lost no opportunity of seeking to check-mate them. The game was played by foes in deadly earnest. When therefore in 1774 the Quebec Act was passed by the British Government, virtually establishing the Roman Catholic Church, the French Civil Law and the French language upon the continent, it became a grievous irritant to the American colonies then in the incipient stage of revolt, and the aggravation was heightened by the extension of the boundaries of the province to the far West, made with the definite purpose of encircling the thirteen colonies by French settlements. As we have seen, the Americans found themselves hemmed in on the North and on the West by traditionary foes and by a civilization with which they could not come to terms. Of course Carleton realised that they would be quick to detect and resent this policy, but none the less did he carry it out, and that of set purpose to counteract if possible the republican tendencies from the colonies which he knew well to his cost were spreading.

These ordinances (he wrote) have been framed upon the principle of securing the dependence of this province (Quebec) upon Great Britain, of suppressing that spirit of licentiousness and independence that has pervaded all the British colonies upon this continent, and was making, through the endeavours of a turbulent faction here, a most amazing progress in this country[1].

He hoped, therefore, by restoring as far as possible the status of affairs that existed under the old regime to gather the noblesse, the seigneurs and the clergy around him, and to cement them by loyalty into a bulwark against the attacks which he feared would soon be made upon them from the South. And in this hope he was not disappointed, though he incensed the British traders and merchants of Quebec, and laid the train for future trouble even among the loyalists who shortly afterwards took refuge in Canada.

It must be kept in mind that these loyalists had been Americans and had gone through a long period of training in constitutional problems. They brought with them ideas which they had learned in their old home, they were anything but docile people, and

[1] Quoted by W. P. M. Kennedy, *Constitution of Canada*, p. 73.

among them were all shades of opinion. Before and
during the War many of them had protested against
the actions of Parliament, of British officials and of
army officers, and they differed from their fellow
Americans chiefly in the strength of their sympathies,
and in the distance which they would be willing to go
in maintaining what they regarded as their constitutional rights. Undoubtedly the mercantile theory of
Empire had caused estrangement, and socially the
peoples of Britain and America had drifted apart, but
the rock on which the unity of the Empire at that time
was wrecked was the constitutional issue[1]. Taxation
as such did not oppress them any more than it did
John Hampden. It was what taxation involved that
aroused their opposition. There had really emerged
for the first time the problem of the Constitution of
the British Empire, the kernel of which was the right
of the Parliament of Great Britain to govern these
colonies. The most advanced leaders openly challenged its prerogatives, holding that the colonies had
been founded by royal charter and that they owed
allegiance only to the King. The Commonwealth,
they held, was one, in the sense that everywhere
Englishmen had the same rights as to the British
Constitution and that this itself was based upon the
natural rights of man. In support of their view they

[1] On this whole matter see C. H. McIlwain, *The American
Revolution.*

cited the instances of the freedom of the Channel Islands, the Isle of Man and Ireland. In other words, they refused to accept Parliament as an Imperial Parliament. We have heard much like this of late and had thought that these were ideas of the twentieth century, but they abound in the political writings of Americans of the eighteenth century.

Chatham and Burke did not agree with the Americans in theory: they held that Parliament had a legal and constitutional right to impose its will upon the colonies, but that it would be politically criminal were it to do so. From their point of view the controversy resolved itself into a matter of practical statesmanship; had their advice been accepted and tact prevailed in England, a compromise might have resulted and the radical American thinkers would not have been able to go to the extreme. Had Americans been allowed to regulate their own affairs and to impose internal taxation they would probably have been content, at least temporarily, to let Britain regulate trade and defence, for they admitted that these were external to themselves and concerned the Empire as a whole.

When rebellion broke out the loyalists, as has been said, did not go so far as the radical Americans. Revolt against Britain they would not, but many of them held the general view, so much under discussion, that they should exercise all the rights of

Englishmen and especially have control of their own local affairs. And in the second Quebec Act of 1791 definite assertion is made that in view of what had happened in the United States the British Parliament would not impose any internal tax or duty for internal revenue, which matter would be dealt with by provincial Assemblies. It would, however, still regulate navigation and commerce for the benefit of the Empire. But this Act laid down definitely the principle of the supremacy of the Imperial Parliament, which the American colonists had challenged. Among English-speaking people of Canada this Act was regarded as not having gone far enough, even strong loyalists desiring a fuller control than it gave them of their own affairs. However, the second great event in the history of the Canadian people intervened before the constitutional discussion became acute.

By all those Americans, and they were not a few, who were of Jefferson's opinion that, as he expressed it in 1808, it was one of the objects of the Government "to exclude all European influence from this hemisphere," the existence of the British colonies was resented as a challenge to this supremacy. For behind them stood Great Britain with her remarkable recuperative power. Canada has often felt the repercussion of American dislike for Britain, but in the War of 1812–4 a deadly blow was aimed at herself and the iron then entered her soul. The campaigns of those years are almost forgotten in England and are of inglorious memory for the United States, but by English-speaking Canadians they are held to be the second most important factor in their national career. It was a war that should not have been fought. Britain did not want it, nor did New York, and the New England states were so bitterly opposed to it that they talked of seceding from the Union; but in spite of the disapproval of the best people Henry Clay carried President Madison with him, having won him over to the hope that England, then in a life and death struggle with Napoleon, could not successfully resist them and that as a consequence Canada would fall into their possession.

It is absurd (said Clay) to suppose that we will not succeed. We have the Canadas as much under our command as Great Britain has the ocean, and the way to conquer her on the ocean is to drive her from the land. I am not for stopping at Quebec or anywhere else; but I would take the whole continent from her and ask no favours[1].

The Hon. John W. Foster admits that the American attitude towards Britain in 1812 was ungenerous, engaged as she then was in defending the liberal principles and institutions which were essential for the well-being of the United States no less than her own; but he goes on to say that "the results of the

---

[1] *Canada and its Provinces*, III, pp. 195 f.

War as a whole may be regarded as of much benefit to the country[1]." To a Canadian this seems a singularly narrow view. Surely naval efficiency and a demonstration that the people would take up arms in a common cause were small gains as against the estrangement for generations of two peoples speaking the same tongue and inheriting a common civilization.

The American aggressors expected a comparatively easy task because they hoped that their old friends who had in recent years settled in Canada would rise and paralyze the activities of the loyalists. But in this they were disappointed. French and English rallied to repel a common foe who had invaded their homes. They were united for the first time in a common cause and the fields of victory have become centres of tradition for both. Of course, success would have been impossible for the Canadians but for the presence of British troops and but for the British fleet on the high seas. If in 1776 the Americans rose in defence of their freedom it was now the turn of the Canadians to defend their rights against the sons of liberty. Pioneers who had suffered for their political faith in 1783 found themselves or their children compelled by the same people to fight a second time for their lives. They knew that they were making a last stand for Britain on the continent;

[1] *A Century of American Diplomacy*, p. 248.

if they were conquered there was an end to British influence. So they fought desperately and held their own. Undefeated they emerged with a new spirit; Canadian sentiment was greatly strengthened and the provinces were to remain a part of the British Empire.

The Maritime provinces had little to complain of from the New Englanders, and their memories of the War have never been keen, but the loyalist of Canada still remembers it. For years afterwards a bitter note recurs in the records of the pioneers; they found the Americans in their midst uncongenial and distrusted them as annexationists, and they were afraid of their support even in the struggle for responsible government. Indeed, reaction against American influence led many moderate men who feared that the Reformers and their sympathizers might adopt republicanism, to espouse the cause of the anti-reform party, critical though they were of its policies.

During the period of agitation for responsible government which followed, the provinces were in perpetual turmoil. The old machinery was out of date and would not work properly, and small cliques at the centres of government kept their hands on it on the plea that this was the best machine available and that they were the only persons competent to run it. They got the ear of most of the governors and of the Colonial Office in London, who were afraid that

if they changed the machinery and gave more freedom a new crew might head the provinces for independence. To a reader of American history it is a
strikingly familiar story, and there can be little doubt
but that the colonial history and the example of their
prosperous self-governing neighbour gave urgency to
the demand of the Reformers. Fortunately Canada,
unlike the United States, had in her years of crisis
some governors of great wisdom and vision, such
as Durham, Sydenham, Bagot and Elgin, though
English statesmen at home were slow to learn the
lesson of the American colonies.

Before the close of this chapter in Canadian history
annexation is heard as a new note. Strange to say,
the suggestion was first made seriously by Canadian
Tories of Montreal, and the fact is significant that the
movement was due to economic distress; for indeed
the successive reappearances of the idea have been
traceable to those whose fortunes have seemed to be
critical or past recovery. The introduction of the
Free-Trade policy by England had brought disaster
to the merchants of Canada, three-fourths of whom
were said to have become bankrupt. After the
country had spent immense sums of money on her
railways and canals there was little to be carried on
them for export to England, and what there was
might easily be diverted to the United States. In
addition to all this the "loyalist" party was angered

at the government for passing the "Rebellion Losses Bill" to indemnify those, chiefly French-Canadians, who had taken part in the Insurrection of 1837, and at the British government for having sanctioned it. England seemed to have lost interest in them; some years before, in 1842, Parliament had confirmed the Ashburton treaty, and not a few of her public men had advised them to cut the painter. Resentment therefore against England, impetuous and transient, not prompted by real or abiding attachment to the United States, vented itself in 1849 in a manifesto for annexation. It was signed in Montreal by many leading merchants, magistrates, lawyers, officers of the militia and even men holding commissions under the Crown, some of whom afterwards, having repented of their indiscretion, held high positions in the public life of Canada. Montreal was the centre of a wide propaganda directed through newspapers and by special agents which secured a good many adherents to the cause in the eastern townships of Quebec, some in western Canada and a few even in New Brunswick. It is difficult to estimate how deep-seated the feeling was, for politics were soon introduced. In western Ontario the Reformers, led by the Hon. Robert Baldwin, came out strongly against the manifesto, but the radical wing of his party called the Clear Grits, having been inclined by American influence to republicanism, united with some Tories in its support. The mass of the people, however, in Canada West, and the overwhelming multitude of the French in Quebec, led by the Church, were unwilling to sell their traditions for the greater commercial prosperity that annexation might bring. They could not, moreover, forget the existence of slavery, to them a repellent feature in the life of their neighbours. It is also to be borne in mind that the American people regarded the proposal with coldness, the South being strongly opposed to the addition of non-slave territory to the Union, and that, though some leading papers in the East were eager for annexation, the government acted with absolute propriety in the matter. Disappointment at the apathy of their neighbours, the emergence of the slavery question and reviving confidence among the Canadians led to the collapse of the project[1]. It had one important result, in leading to the successful negotiation of a Reciprocity treaty by Lord Elgin, who believed that the only way of avoiding repetition of the movement was "to put the colonists in as good a position commercially as the citizens of the United States in order to which free navigation and reciprocal trade with the United States were indispensable."

The new idea of modern imperialism was born in this confusion. Some English statesmen, irritated

[1] C. D. Allin and Jones, *Annexation, Preferential Trade and Reciprocity*, p. 358.

doubtless by the constant difficulties occasioned by the friction between the British provinces and the United States and pessimistic as to their future, had come to believe that it was merely a matter of time when their connection with the Mother Land would cease; indeed, Lord John Russell publicly stated that he looked forward to their becoming independent of England. This utterance was greatly resented by Lord Elgin and the Hon. Robert Baldwin, who complained bitterly that such views were ammunition for the annexationists. Lord Elgin took the Colonial Secretary roundly to task for thus stifling the great possibilities of Canada and the Empire:

> You must renounce the habit of telling the colonies that the colonial is a provisional existence. You must allow them to believe that without severing the bonds which unite them to Great Britain they may attain the degree of perfection and of social and political development to which organized communities of free men have a right to aspire[1].

Unpopular though he was with a section of the Canadian people, Elgin is now recognized as not only one of the greatest governors but as a pre-eminent figure in the creation of the modern British Empire.

The Civil War could not fail to have a great influence on the development of Canadian nationality. Its general effect was to create in the northern states a hostile attitude towards Canada for her supposedly

[1] Allin, *op. cit.* p. 282.

active sympathy with the South, and to deepen in Canada the fear lest the provinces if they remained disunited would succumb to the superior power of an unfriendly neighbour. As a matter of fact the governments of the provinces were consistently correct in their attitude, and the great majority of the people were antecedently favourable to the North, as is shown by their enlistments which Goldwin Smith estimated at 40,000, not because they had any special interest in the struggle for the maintenance of the Union, but because they abhorred slavery and they knew that its abolition was the real aim of Lincoln and his party. In the provinces *Uncle Tom's Cabin* had made almost as strong an appeal to the emotions of the English and Scotch population as to the puritans of New England, and northern sympathizers found their spokesmen in the Hon. George Brown, then at the height of his power as editor of the Toronto *Globe*, and in the Hon. D'Arcy McGee, who strongly upheld the cause of the North. In 1861 Lincoln assured the Hon. A. T. Galt, a member of the Canadian Cabinet, that "for himself and his Cabinet he had never heard from one of his ministers a hostile expression towards us, and he pledged himself as a man of honour that neither he nor his Cabinet entertained the slightest aggressive designs upon Canada, nor had any desire to disturb the rights of Great Britain on this continent." Yet before that administration had come into office Seward had advocated the annexation of Canada as a compensation for such losses as they might incur from the South.

This generally favourable attitude continued at least until the *Trent* affair; but by December 1861 Canadians realised that during the winter they would likely have to bear the brunt of an invasion. Naturally this caused a great revulsion of feeling, which was heightened by the threats of the American press. Palmerston, Russell, Gladstone and the *Times* may have been wrong in their attitude towards the North. Canadians knew little or nothing of their policies, nor did they necessarily follow their judgments. It was no longer with them a question of sympathy with North or South. They now saw that their own political existence was endangered. They knew that the United States had always treated it as a temporary inconvenience and that they might have to fight for their life at tremendous odds. Therefore they set themselves in an attitude of defence, transportation by canal and railway was greatly improved, and troops came out from England.

When this incident blew over the situation had changed. Sympathisers with the South there had always been in the cities, and these were reinforced by an inflow of southern families and of others, especially into the Maritime provinces, who made fortunes by supplying the blockade-runners which eluded the northern ships, and who became vocal[1]. We know only too well how people who are fighting desperately interpret neutrality as being almost equivalent to hostility and any suggestion of sympathy with the foe as unpardonable. Correctness of official attitude will not atone for the indiscretions of individuals. It was therefore to be expected that the North would magnify the comfort ministered to the enemy and convict the British provinces of unfriendliness. Russell, the correspondent of the *Times*, agreed with other observers that after the war the Federal armies might attempt to over-run and annex Canada. A bill was actually introduced into the House of Representatives providing for the admission of the British provinces into the Union. Even when the war was over the storm still threatened the Canadian border, and the Fenian raids broke like angry flashes; nor would the American government make any compensation for the damages which Canadians had suffered from their disbanded soldiers.

It was a hard time for those who clung to the hope that the British provinces would maintain their existence in connection with the Mother Country. They knew that most of the American leaders would sweep away if they could every vestige of British rule from the continent, and instead of being encouraged at such a moment by support from the English govern-

[1] Landon, *Canadian Historical Review*, I, 3 and III, 1.

ment they had chilling responses from some of those in power. "With a view, probably, to the satisfaction of mortified friends of the North in England, Mr Gladstone wrote me," says Goldwin Smith, "suggesting, if the North thought fit to let the South go, it might in time be indemnified by the union of Canada with the northern states[1]." This school of Englishmen regarded American jealousy as not only a source of recurrent diplomatic trouble but a menace to the good relations between Britain and the United States. Goldwin Smith himself was always "the Bystander" in respect of Canada, and was contemptuous of the prevalent idealism which in his judgment opposed a futile resistance to its economic destiny. He really did not understand the land of his domicile. How far the people have journeyed since those days if, as seems to be the case, the Dominion of Canada is becoming a bond of unity between the two sections of the English-speaking world.

It was well for Canada that other views prevailed in Britain at the close of the Civil War, for the victory of the North left her in a state of conscious weakness, and if she had been persuaded that Britain would not make vigorous opposition to aggressive action from the United States the heart might have gone out of her entirely. Her fears of the American did not die down. Something said or done would revive them

[1] *My Memory of Gladstone*, p. 43.

every now and then. In 1866 the Reciprocity treaty was abrogated, for which, however, Canada was partly to blame. In 1868 Seward stated that he hoped that the purchase of Alaska from Russia would result in the expulsion of Britain from the Pacific coast, and that the absorption of British Columbia in the United States would hasten the manifest destiny of Canada. Sumner also sounded an alarm by a speech in which he suggested that Britain could only pay for the losses she had inflicted upon America during the Civil war by handing over all her possessions on the North American continent to the Government of the United States; and that this was no passing petulance is shown by the fact that he wrote in the same year in a similar strain to Hamilton Fish, the Secretary of State, believing, as the Hon. J. W. Foster remarks, "in common with many of the most far-sighted of our public men—Franklin, John Adams, Seward and others—that the greatest menace to our peace with Great Britain was in the maintenance of a colonial dependency on our northern border[1]."

Confederation was the reply of the British provinces to these suggestions. Though there is much truth in Goldwin Smith's aphorism that "the real parent of Confederation was Deadlock," self-protection was also a strong motive in its creation. In

[1] *Op. cit.* pp. 428 f.

the thrust and parry between the United States and
Britain scattered provinces might come to harm; con-
federated they would acquire strength and higher
status. Had the provinces not been united in 1867
they would possibly by this time have been absorbed
one by one into the United States.

The idea of Federation was by no means novel. It
had been in the air before the American Revolution,
a similar experiment having been proposed for those
colonies in 1754 when twenty-five delegates met at
Albany to consider "union and confederation." In
general the colonial legislature was to control its own
domestic affairs, levy its own taxes and make its own
laws subject to an appeal to the Crown. Had this
proposal become effective the constitutional difficulty
might have been solved and Canada's place in history
might have been very different; but every colonial
Assembly rejected the measure; they would not
unite, nor would they accept unity imposed upon
them by England. All this sounds very familiar to
one who knows the process whereby the Canadian
Confederation came into being. There appeared a
similar disinclination on the part of the provinces to
unite, Ontario and Quebec having been forced together
by reason of an impasse, New Brunswick having
entered reluctantly, Nova Scotia remaining rebellious
for years against the constraint that was laid upon her.

Canadian statesmen knew well the difficulties in

which after the Revolution the constitution of the
United States had been cradled; they knew also that
one object of the terrible Civil war had been to ensure
that in future the centripetal federal forces should
prevail over the individualism of states or groups of
states. With these facts in mind the fathers of Confederation provided that in the new Dominion the
centre should control the destinies of the people as a
whole. Sir John Macdonald actually wished a legis-
lative union of the provinces, but the character of
Quebec made this impossible. The powers of the
central government were defined as were those of the
provinces, but the residue for the "peace, order and
good government of Canada" went to the Dominion.
Canada is more than an aggregation of sovereign
provinces; Ottawa is the active seat of unifying legislation and executive control through the largest
national issues. It is hardly open to question that
this result, in such contrast to the constitution of the
United States, was due in large measure to the well-
known experience through which the Americans had
passed.

Their difficulties also in respect of inter-state trade,
transportation, law and order were warnings of what
should be avoided by men who were making a new
federation. Not only was this prudent as regards the
original provinces, but by the year 1867 it was
evident that the future of Canada would depend upon

the character of the Great West with which inter-communication also was a vital necessity. In the original constitution of the United States there was no federal authority outside of the States to organize and direct new territories, therefore after the Louisiana Purchase in 1803 the question arose whether the national government had authority to build roads and develop internal improvements at national expense. In fact, such questions had arisen earlier and divided parties. Similar questions arose in Canada before Confederation and led to the conferring on the central government of the power to control new territories and to unify the provinces by the establishment of common law and order and by providing for their commercial and industrial needs. In the British North America Act, therefore, all matters of trade and commerce, transportation and banking were put under the authority of the Dominion Parliament, whereas in the United States such unification as has been achieved in respect of these matters has been slow and the process often devious. Criminal law also was placed within the jurisdiction of Ottawa, so that it is the same for every part of the Dominion, and the Canadian people are well satisfied with the record of their courts. Competing jurisdictions in the United States have been the cause of interminable delays and many miscarriages[1].

[1] Z. A. Lash, *The Federation of Canada*, pp. 86 ff.

It cannot be denied that the Americans were unpleasantly surprised at the consummation of Confederation and did not take kindly to the new Dominion of Canada. In it a new imperial problem was supplied for them on their northern border[1]. They were slow to recognize the large measure of autonomy with which Britain had equipped the new State for her voyage. It is well known, for example, how hardly Sir John Macdonald was given recognition in the Fisheries Negotiations in 1871 at Washington and how annoyed the Americans were at the deference paid him by the British plenipotentiaries. Even at home he found traces of American interference with his policies. He was convinced that influences emanating from Washington had been at work to checkmate the Dominion in its negotiations to secure possession of the North-West Territories from the Hudson's Bay Company, and that unneighbourly support had been given at the time of the Riel Rebellion in 1869. Probably the enterprise that caused him most anxiety was the Canadian Pacific Railway, for on its construction depended the success of Confederation, but he discovered in 1870 that the Northern Pacific

[1] Sir John Macdonald wrote to Lord Knutsford in 1889 that in the Canadian draft of the Bill of Confederation the title *Kingdom* was used instead of *Dominion*, and that the change was made at the instance of Lord Derby, then Foreign Minister, who feared that the form would wound the susceptibilities of the Americans.

Railway had been built near the border with branches running north by persons working in concert with the government "to injure, if not prevent, the construction of an independent line in British territory[1]."

Macdonald was the first pilot to take the Canadian ship of state out into the open, and he had to thread many a perilous channel. He was not even certain of his crew, and the crew had little confidence in one another; the French were suspicious of Ontario, Nova Scotia was sulking, the North-West was just recovering from rebellion, her future uncertain. Intensely attached to British institutions, he had to prove that these scattered and diverse provinces could endure as part of the Empire. It is no matter of surprise, therefore, that in 1888 he resented as an insult Senator Sherman's symptomatic proposal to buy Canada. To the end of his days he was suspicious of the Americans, or even embittered towards them. He wrote to his old friend Stephen in 1890, "Tupper will tell you that every American statesman (and he saw them all in '88) covets Canada. The greed for its acquisition is still on the increase and God knows where it will end[2]."

In fairness to the United States it must be borne in mind that she was not yet sure of herself. The effects of the Civil war had not worn off, people of

---

[1] *Correspondence of Sir John A. Macdonald* (1921), p. 124.
[2] *Op. cit.* p. 478.

all sorts had fled to her for refuge and were nursing their discontents against Europe, and the outside world was not friendly towards her. At such a time, irritated and disillusioned, not yet having acquired the confident step of one who had attained, nor having distinguished between size and quality, it was natural that she should look askance upon the appearance on her borders of a new Confederacy within the British Empire which might in the future dispute her omnipotence on the continent.

Macdonald's great successor, after an interval of five years, was Sir Wilfrid Laurier. He was a genuine French-Canadian and grew in devotion to his people as the years went by. Though he was in spirit a Whig and took the English Liberals as his models, he had none of Macdonald's emotional attachment to Britain. Moreover, he had been forced by the political manœuvres of Sir John Macdonald to assume a more friendly attitude than he did towards the United States; but he was not as much influenced by American methods in politics as were some of his English-speaking colleagues. When he came into power in 1896 a change had come over the relations of the United States to Canada, and, as Mr James Ford Rhodes says, "those who believed in the expansion of the United States to cover the whole of America became fewer and less blatant." Mr Bayard as Secretary of State under Mr Cleveland hoped by freer

trade to create an abiding friendship based upon
common prosperity, and Cleveland, in forwarding a
draft treaty to the Senate, which, however, they rejected, used these memorable words: "Mutual advantage and convenience are the only permanent
foundation of peace and friendship between States."
Officially the air at Washington was more genial to
Canada, especially in the Secretaryship of John
Hay, of whom Laurier wrote home: "If the Senate
sometimes irritates us, it irritates the Secretary of
State still more." But it was an April sky, that of
the United States, in Laurier's regime—sun and
showers. With resolute good-will he tried to trade
with them but he found them hard bargainers; he
was met by the Dingley Tariff and with dignity
he turned to England and offered her the Preference.
When once again in 1911 he sought to trade, and
accepted the offer of Mr Taft to have reciprocity,
he found to his amazement that the Canadians
agreed with Speaker Champ Clark's indiscreet utterance that reciprocity would lead to annexation,
and that nine-tenths of the American people would
have it so. Therefore the majority rejected it
and Laurier went out of power. On the whole it
may be said that his regime was one of increasing
friendliness to the United States, though no inconsiderable factor in the situation was the better
feeling that had been growing between the United

States and Great Britain since the Spanish war of 1898.

The most serious set-back to good relations in this period was caused by Mr Cleveland's message to Congress in 1896 on the Venezuelan controversy. To-day Cleveland appears to have been fatuous in jeopardizing good relations with Britain by invoking the Monroe Doctrine in a minor boundary dispute between Great Britain and such an unstable republic as Venezuela then was, and that in the face of the opposition of such friends as Thomas F. Bayard and Edward J. Phelps. The flame of jingoism that burst out over the United States on the publication of the message showed how much inflammable material there still was lying around. Some who were not as a rule unfriendly critics of England saw shifting intrigues shaping themselves on the surface of British diplomacy; and Mr J. Ford Rhodes, who disagreed with Cleveland's action, traces such agreement with it as was found among the more intelligent classes to inveterate suspicion[1]. The Canadian on his part realized once more how easily his neighbour might be excited against the Empire of which he was a part and how much less secure he was than he had assumed himself to be. Until then he had accepted the view that the Monroe Doctrine, having been assented to by Great Britain, was good enough for him, but

[1] *History of the United States*, vol. 1877–96, pp. 448–454.

Mr Olney's message put it in a new light. If, as he said, "the United States is practically sovereign on this continent, and its fiat is law upon the subjects to which it confines its interposition," then Professor Coolidge is right that "the theory of a natural separation between the new world and the old is an essential part of the reasoning on which the Monroe Doctrine is based[1]." But this was to ignore the unique place which Canada had come to hold as a self-governing unit in a Commonwealth of which the members are spread in every quarter of the globe. Old and new in this organism are blended into one; Canada's life-blood and her inheritance are in large part drawn from Britain; she shares these with her sister nations, and to Britain all gladly own their loyalty. To-day the United States does not stand on the Americas as the leader of young nations who look to her for protection against Europe. It is doubtful if the Latin republics of the southern hemisphere would willingly accept her as protectress, and of course since the Great War they do not fear that an aggressive old world will interpose in the affairs of the new.

Over against the United States now stands in friendly intercourse the Britannic Commonwealth with rapidly developing members on the American continents—Canada, the British West Indies and

[1] A. C. Coolidge, *The United States as a World Power*, p. 117.

British Guiana. It may be that a second Federation will be brought into existence consisting of the latter two sections, and if so this Federation would in all probability be closely connected with Canada in commerce and in other friendly relations. In many of their products and in their trade these islands and Guiana are complementary to Canada. They export sugar, cacao, fruits, asphalt, and perhaps before long they will supply cotton; they take northern fish, wheat and manufactured goods. Now that the Panama Canal is opened they are equally easy of access to the eastern or to the western coast. They cannot fail to play an important part in Canada's future. If a dispute were to arise with one of the Caribbean republics of such proportions as to demand the intervention of Britain as the head of a Commonwealth of nations, would the United States step in and assert her sole right to settle it? This was what she did in the Venezuelan matter. But in the future Canada might have very great interest in the solution. Foreign policy is rapidly becoming an affair not of Britain alone but of the Britannic Commonwealth.

In so far as the Monroe Doctrine refers to Brazil, the Argentine, Chili and Peru, Canada would probably stand aside; it is the future of the West Indies that concerns her. If it should ever happen that any of the Islands now owned by other European nations should become saleable, the Canadian might find his own interests leading him to urge Britain to purchase it, and he might be unwilling to admit that the Monroe Doctrine should be invoked to prevent the acquisition. He therefore welcomes the recent interpretation of the Doctrine made by Mr Hughes, late Secretary of State, that "It is not a policy of aggression but of self-defence and an assertion of the principle of national security," and as set forth again by him at a meeting of the American Bar Association in 1923:

> The sentiment of the American people is practically unanimous that in the interest of our national safety we could not yield to any foreign power the control of the Panama Canal, or the approaches to it, or the obtaining of any position which would interfere with our right of protection or would menace the freedom of our communications.

Mr Taft also said some years ago in Toronto that the heart of the Doctrine was the exclusion of menacing foreign influence from the Caribbean Sea. Nothing that Canada could reasonably ask for would run counter to this principle. Next to the United States she is the nation most interested in the protection of the zones around the Panama Canal. Americans also will understand that the interest of the Canadians in the West Indies is second only to their own. These two peoples which have learned "the habit of peace," to use Secretary Hughes's words, are not likely henceforward to act unreasonably in any incident in which the Monroe Doctrine will come into play.

A century of unbroken peace between America and Britain was celebrated in 1915, though on account of the War the occasion passed by without attracting much notice. But it should otherwise have called forth expressions of thankfulness and of high resolve to perpetuate the habit, for it is evident from what has been already said that once or twice the skating was on very thin ice. One of the most notable instances of international sanity throughout this period was the maintenance of the Rush-Bagot Agreement which has been in effect since 1817. By it the two governments agreed to keep on Lake Ontario only one vessel each of one hundred tons armed with one eighteen-pounder; two vessels of similar size and armament on the upper Lakes, and one of the same style and armed strength on Lake Champlain. Attempts have been made by ship-builders to have the agreement repealed, but still it stands, having been relaxed only during the Great War when Canada agreed that the United States should be allowed to have a dozen or more ships of war so armed as to give adequate training to recruits enlisted for the national forces. This has been a triumph for reasonable relationships and it attracted very favourable comment at the Washington Conference on Disarmament.

Though the Great War interfered with the due celebration of one hundred years of peace, it did far

more than any commemorations could have effected
in changing the attitude of each country to the other.
It goes without saying at this time that the common
purpose and the common sacrifice opened the eyes of
Canada to the privilege of her position in the British
Commonwealth; but none the less did it antiquate
the view expressed by Professor Coolidge in 1908:
"It is a fact of the present that the drawing together
of Great Britain and Canada is in no sense to the
benefit of the United States[1]." Apparently this view
was based on the assumption that Canada was a hostile
neighbour whose attitude was so fixed that nothing
but annexation could change it. To-day the American
of Anglo-Saxon stock does not talk to his Canadian
neighbour about annexation. He has discovered that
Canada has a real individuality. He admired her
action in the War, he was proud of what one so like
himself and so close beside him did on the battlefields
of Europe, and he is pondering as never before what
her destiny may be. That is not to say that he yet
understands her position; he has hardly grasped the
meaning of autonomy within the Empire.

Objection was taken in the American Congress to
the place given at the Versailles Peace Conference to
the representatives of the Dominions, and the Senate
of the United States has not yet admitted the status
of Canada. At the time the opinion was widespread

[1] *Op. cit.* p. 263.

in the American Press that it was a token of independence and would soon result in the disruption of the Empire. But the Hon. N. W. Rowell, who had much to do with the securing of the position for the Dominions, has put the case well:

> Article I of the Covenant of the League provides "Any full self-governing State, Dominion or Colony may become a member of the League." This provision appears to have been overlooked by those who think that membership of the Dominions in the League is a step towards separation. It is just the reverse. Membership on the conditions named means that the other nations have recognized the unique character of the Britannic Commonwealth and have admitted the Dominions to the family of nations without involving separation or even the idea of separation from the parent State[1].

Nor was this participation by the Dominions a formal matter. Canada sided with the United States in the discussion of Article X, one of the most contested of all, reserving for herself the right to have her Parliament pronounce on the advisability of the Dominion taking part in any external conflict. Was she not in this giving expression to the common North American point-of-view? She also asserted successfully the new principle in taking her place at the Disarmament Conference at Washington, though she had received no invitation from the United States, inasmuch as the Senate, not having become a party to

[1] *The British Empire and World Peace*, p. 179.

the League, had not formally acknowledged the claim of the Dominions.

A further noteworthy change was made by the Canadian Government in concluding a Halibut Fisheries Treaty with the United States in 1923. This settled a question which arose out of the treaty of 1818. The Senate of the United States had placed almost prohibitive duties on Canadian halibut and other fresh fish, even on fish caught by Americans and shipped in bond through Canadian territory. The Canadian government replied by prohibiting the selling of bait to American fishermen in Canadian waters unless they delivered their catches in Canadian ports. Our present interest in the treaty, however, lies in the fact that it was signed at Washington by the Canadian Minister of Marine and Fisheries and not by the Ambassador of Great Britain to the United States. The Canadian government urged that it was a domestic affair, and after due exchange of views the words "Great Britain" were deliberately omitted from the treaty, which runs "Convention for the Regulation of Halibut Fisheries on the Pacific Coast of Canada and the United States." The American Senate accepted the signature of the Canadian representative on the understanding that it would bind all British subjects and so be applicable not merely to Canada but, as former British treaties, to the whole Empire. In consequence, this policy has been formulated: Any Dominion government may advise the King directly to issue full powers to its representative in negotiating such treaties as relate solely to its domestic affairs, which he will do after consulting his Ministers in Great Britain, but the Dominion that intends to negotiate must notify the associated governments so that they may decide whether any of their interests are sufficiently involved to require their presence at the negotiations. By such action Canada exercises one of the chief prerogatives of a nation as far as her own interests are concerned, and the United States has made no objection to this direct negotiation, though of course neither government can overlook the fact that the King before issuing such powers to Canada has taken the advice of his Imperial government.

All this leads up to another position which has been prepared for but not yet occupied, the appointment of a Canadian representative at Washington. For years the greatest portion of the British Ambassador's duties have concerned the Dominion of Canada, but owing to the procedure there have been frequent delays and misunderstandings. As far back as 1888 Sir Charles Tupper wrote to Sir John Macdonald that if he had his way he would get the British Government to send Macdonald as Minister to Washington "to show us in the most striking manner the fixed determination to make our interests the paramount consideration[1]." Though this idea was different from that which may soon be acted upon, it was prompted by the same underlying cause.

The British Commonwealth has been rapidly assuming a new character, and it is not strange that the Americans should wonder what its constitution is and with whom they are dealing. The government of Britain they have known. Though they often distrusted her diplomacy they accepted an agreement with her diplomats as final. But what status have these erstwhile Canadian provincials in the enforcement of any treaty that they may negotiate in the King's name? Will the Imperial Parliament stand behind it, giving it the prestige of an Imperial engagement? The situation is novel and there are inconsistencies in theory and action, but doubtless President Lowell speaks for thoughtful Americans in these words:

It is inconceivable that any branch of the United States government should seek intentionally to exert an influence, direct or indirect, on the organization of the British Empire, or the relation of each other to its component parts; still less that it should strive to prevent a relaxation in the guardianship of Great Britain over Canada[2].

Canada has travelled a long distance since the view prevailed in the United States that she was in thral-

---

[1] *Op. cit.* p. 432.
[2] *Foreign Affairs*, II, I, p. 22.

dom to Britain and that annexation would soon bring her deliverance. It cannot be truly said that annexation was ever a live issue in Canadian politics, even at the period when "Unrestricted reciprocity"[1] was taken up by Liberals. There have been sporadic suggestions that the domestic difficulties between the English and the French might issue in this result. Lord Durham said long ago in his Report that the antipathy between the two races was so strong in the lower province that the British minority rather than be ruled by the French would join the United States. The suggestion flared up again at the time of the Jesuits' Estates Agitation in 1889, but it was a flash due to disappointed vehemence rather than to the permanent heat of racial friction, and the relations between the French and the English are better at present than they have ever been.

In the United States also little is heard to-day of Canada's manifest destiny, for most people are much less certain than they were that it is so manifest. When President Harding visited British Columbia, a few days before his death, he was the first American president to pay an official visit to the Dominion, and he was received, as the press said, with a welcome that no other ruler than King George himself would have been given, as the representative of a people with virtually the same ideals and institutions. His speech,

[1] See p. 151.

therefore, had peculiar significance, and of all his friendly words none touched the Canadian more than those in which he said, "the bugaboo of annexation having become extinct long ago ...... let us go our own gait along parallel roads: you helping us and we helping you."

In accounting for the change the remarkable economic development of both countries during the last generation must not be overlooked. The United States has grown to be the richest and most powerful nation in the world. No longer is she sensitive lest she do not get recognition, nor does she desire to extend her imperial obligations. She does not challenge the place of the British Commonwealth in the world; in fact she is being criticized for having fastened her gaze so completely upon her own domestic interests. Moreover, Canada has made a success of her great experiment; she has even assumed a place in the world's Council Chamber, where the United States has so far refused to take a seat, and, as we proceed to show, has thriven commercially. The Ship of State is not drifting on the tide, to be cast helplessly upon her neighbour's shores, but is directing her own course as one of a fleet of vessels keeping together on a great expedition.

CHAPTER V

Trade and Commerce

DURING the latter part of the nineteenth century the scattered provinces of the Dominion found themselves in a very difficult position by reason of their contiguity to a large and prosperous nation. They were thinly settled and poor. With no great cities to supply markets for their farmers they had to seek foreign outlets for their natural products; in winter only two of their ports were open, Halifax and St John, and these were so distant from the centre of population that the upper provinces conducted most of their trade, while the St Lawrence was closed, through the ports of Portland and Boston. The United States, however, their advantageously placed neighbour, was continuously settled, a full stream of immigration was pouring in, cities were rapidly building and her abundant resources and varieties of climate were such that the needs and supplies of the sections of the country were complementary to one another; and her markets she kept to herself. But the Americans also sought foreign markets for their trade, most of which consisted of natural products similar to those of Canada, and they shipped all the year round from their ports. Whatever wealth Canada earned in the last century was in competition with a rival so much better situated than herself that she had time and again a hard struggle for her existence. It cannot be said that the United States was ever generous to her in trade; Canada has always taken far more from her than she sent to her, and would not have been able to make such heavy purchases had not Great Britain been a large importer of the products of the Dominion. We do not need, however, to discover any very unneighbourly frame of mind towards Canada in the protectionism of the United States; it was a policy that nearly all other countries but England had adopted; and the nation was still young and had not acquired the quiet assurance that comes with years and hereditary wealth. But Canada wished to trade with the United States, though she found her very unyielding. Why should not her provinces be as prosperous as New York, or at least as Ohio or New England? Why was business so much duller on the one side of the line than on the other? These questions, when put in hard times, brought the suggestion: Shall we secure this prosperity by compromising our independence? It was a severe temptation for Canada when she saw thousands of her best young men and women crossing the border in the hope of employment at higher wages than they could get at home. Within sight was a land of prosperity while her own trade and agriculture were languishing. But often as the temptation has come Canada has averted her eyes, bowed her head and knit her muscles to resume her own self-appointed task. The words of the Hon. A. T. Galt, in his Budget Speech of 1866, might have been spoken in almost any year since then:

> It is desirable, and indeed our manifest duty, to show (the Americans) not in a spirit of hostility, but certainly in that of independence, that while we value their friendship and value their trade, we will not conform to unreasonable terms and will not have either our commercial policy or our political allegiance dictated to us by any foreign country[1].

Apart from the Atlantic Fisheries, hardly any trade question can be said to have existed between the British provinces and the United States until the introduction of Free Trade into England on the abolition of the Corn Laws in 1846 led to great dislocation in Canadian commerce. From the earliest days both the Maritime provinces and Canada had been too dependent upon Great Britian. Unlike the United States, they felt that in her they had one upon whom they had a claim, and this assumption had reduced their initiative. They were still in the colonial stage. After long negotiations the English government had agreed to admit wheat and flour exported from Canadian ports into the home market at the nominal price of one shilling a quarter, while at the same time

[1] Quoted by J. S. Willison, in *Sir Wilfrid Laurier and the Liberal Party*, II, p. 77.

the Canadian legislature placed a duty on American wheat to prevent it from being shipped to England along their waterways and becoming a competitor. American wheat, however, was admitted free when imported to be turned into flour in Canada. This led to an almost mushroom growth of the milling industry in the years immediately preceding 1846. From 1840 onwards the waterways, especially the St Lawrence and the Welland canals, had been opened up at enormous expense to the colonies in the hope that the grain of Upper Canada, and even of the western states as flour, would find its way to the preferential market of Great Britain more cheaply than by the Erie canal, which along with the American railways had taken away much of the trade that had hitherto gone down the St Lawrence. Montreal was building itself on the hope of becoming a great emporium for wheat and flour. To its consternation the Corn Laws and all preferences were repealed in 1846. The disappearance of preferential duties on timber added to the outcry from Halifax to Ottawa, though Canada's supplies in quality and quantity gave her still a great advantage over the United States. To add to the grievances the historic Navigation Laws which confined British trade to British owned and manned vessels were repealed in 1849. The Home government recognized that if they removed preferential duties with the one hand they could not hold them fast against Canadians with the other, and in the hope of encouraging commerce by the St Lawrence route and reducing rates they opened trade to vessels of all nationalities equally. This led, however, to complaints, especially in the Maritime provinces, where there was a large fleet of ships, because they feared the competition of Americans in the West Indies and even in Britain itself.

Canada felt the changed situation keenly. Lord Elgin wrote to the Colonial Secretary in 1848: "Property in most of the Canadian towns, and especially in the Capital, has fallen fifty per cent. in value within the last three years. Three-fourths of the commerical men are bankrupt owing to Free Trade." At this time other domestic difficulties were added like fuel on a rising fire. Since the Rebellion of 1837 there had been in Quebec a clamour for compensation to those who had, not a few of them through their own disloyalty by participating in the uprising, been deprived of their property, and to pacify it the Coalition government had passed the "Rebellion Losses Bill." To the intense indignation of the Tories, Lord Elgin signed the Bill in 1849 and was almost killed by a Montreal mob for his constitutional action. As has been previously stated, the situation culminated in the celebrated annexation manifesto.

England, in abolishing the Corn Laws, knew well what she was doing; hers was a thoroughly considered policy for her own people. As for the rest, Gladstone replied rather cavalierly to the address from Canada with its gloomy forebodings in 1846 that it was much more important that the people of England should have cheap food than that the Empire should become a burden, and that Canada could easily compete with the United States in the British market. He promised, however, that the British government would endeavour to secure some offset to her losses by arranging a reciprocity agreement with Washington. This was no easy task. Much preliminary negotiation and many exchanges of views were necessary to pave the way for it. Emissaries came from Washington to Canada, and Canadians were sent to Washington. But above all it was to Lord Elgin that the final credit was chiefly due. He was convinced that with patience and tact on the part of the British Government the provinces would remain loyal. Restricted trade was the most serious factor in the situation; if prosperity were to revisit Canada little would be heard of annexation. Efforts were made to negotiate a treaty at Washington, but all to no purpose. The favourable elements in Congress were not strong enough, though in 1848 the Secretary of the Treasury had reported that very great advantages would accrue to the United States if a reciprocity agreement were concluded, especially as nearly all surplus Canadian products exported abroad would in these circumstances be carried on American railroads and ships. Senator Dix of New York also was able to show that out of reciprocal trade the United States would have a balance in her favour. But the bill failed to pass the Senate against the opposition of agricultural and manufacturing interests, and especially of the South. However, the tide was about to turn as new influences came into the ascendant. The North was generally favourable to Canada, supported by President Pierce and especially by the able Secretary of State, W. L. Marcy, and New England coveted the Maritime fisheries. But, strange to say, difficulties developed in the Maritime provinces which at that time were fairly prosperous and evinced a fear of being drawn within the orbit of the United States. A memorial was issued in Halifax deprecating concessions to

a power which ever seconds the efforts of astute diplomacy by appeals to the angry passions—the full force of which has been twice on British America within the memory of this generation, and, in a just cause, with the aid of the mother country, could be broken again[1].

They feared the gifts of the Greeks. To meet this situation the American government employed a special agent to whom Marcy gave these instructions:

You will in a proper manner confer with the most influential men in the colonies to express the interest this

[1] Tansill, *op. cit.* p. 67 *n.*

government has in their advancement and its wish to tighten the bonds which unite the two countries[1].

The "proper manner" included not only diplomatic methods but the use of considerable sums of money, which the agent distributed so effectively that there were quick reversals of opinion on the part of editors and legislators in Nova Scotia and New Brunswick[2]. This was one side of the negotiations, a picture creditable neither to the American government nor to some highly placed persons in the Maritime provinces.

The other and more important side was the scene at Washington. Here that prince of diplomats, Lord Elgin himself, took the principal part. At this time the South, in the growing intensity of the slavery struggle, was resisting the Kansas-Nebraska Bill, as it would have resisted any other which would have added power to the white states. Southerners did not want Canada to be annexed. Give her, they said, reciprocity, or any freer trade she asks, to satisfy her. Senator Collamer of Vermont wrote in 1865 that he had said in the Senate that the proposal was made

with a view to quiet the people of Canada and prevent their annexation to the North, which might disturb the "balance of power" of our southern friends, and Mr Toombs (senator from Georgia) then sitting on the other side of the chamber,

[1] Tansill, *op. cit.* p. 62.   [2] *Op. cit.* pp. 70–73.

bowed very low to me and said "We have got the Treaty: they have been quieted[1]."

But Lord Elgin's persuasive powers also were used to great purpose. He was no less eager than the southern democrats to prevent annexation, who along with the favourable northern influences already referred to got the treaty through the Senate in August 1854. By its terms the markets of both countries were to be free to both peoples in grain, flour, animals, meats, vegetables and other products of the farm, in fish, lumber, timber, coal, etc. Though no mention was made of reciprocity in manufactured goods, it was understood that the Canadian tariff, which at that time was low, would be maintained by the Government in accordance with a "most liberal commercial policy." Americans were given the right to navigate the St Lawrence river and the Canadian canals on the same conditions as Canadians, and Canadians to navigate Lake Michigan freely. No export duty was to be levied on lumber cut in the state of Maine and floated down the St John river to its mouth[2].

The effects of the treaty soon became apparent. Trade between the two countries increased rapidly. New channels of commerce were created in different sections, produce finding the market which geographical situation or means of transport made most

---

[1] *Op. cit.* p. 77.　　[2] *Op. cit.* p. 81.

natural. The Maritime Provinces bought their flour from the United States; western Ontario sent its farm output into New York and shipped grain by American waterways to Europe. Out of reciprocity the Americans on the whole got the advantage. Montreal complained that it had gained little. American grain was not going to Europe by the St Lawrence; the United States were supplying the Maritime provinces; manufactures were not being developed. But at this time the prosperity of Canada was being augmented from other sources—the high prices due to the Crimean war, the closing of the grain export from Russia, and the expenditure of capital in the country on the construction of railways. All this gave rise to a movement led by the Hon. A. T. Galt for the increase of duties on manufactured goods, which about six years after the conclusion of the treaty were raised from fifteen to twenty per cent. Canada West did not agree with him, nor the Maritime provinces; and the Americans, not without good reason, protested against the policy as a "violation, not only of the letter and spirit of the treaty, but of the amity and good faith in which it was conceived[1]"; in this also the British Government supported the Americans. But Galt replied, as Minister of Finance, that the primary purpose of the imposition of the duties was to secure revenue to meet the interest on

[1] J. S. Willison, *op. cit.* p. 75.

the immense outlay that had been made on public works, though he admitted that if the duties helped to develop home manufactures, so much the better.

Far more potent, however, for the abrogation of the treaty than this small rise in duties was the changed attitude of the Americans after the Civil War. The North was incensed against the Canadians for the sympathy shown by many of their leaders to the South, and for the money they had made through blockade-running. It resented the prosperity of the British provinces on its border in possession of such valuable natural resources and waterways; and a large body of opinion held that the repeal of reciprocity would force them into annexation. Indeed, Galt said so in his budget speech of 1866:

If there was one thing more than another, apart from the irritation growing out of the events which happened during the late war, which instigated them in abrogating the reciprocity treaty, it was the belief that they could compel us into a closer political alliance with them[1].

The United States was not unanimous in making the repeal. New York protested. Had the Americans played their game skilfully they might possibly have thwarted Confederation, but they were angry and dealt a blow.

By this action the people of the British provinces found their trade dislocated a second time, and

[1] Willison, *op. cit.* II, p. 77.

naturally began to ask whether they could not do something for their mutual protection and benefit. Could they not draw more closely together, and be less dependent upon a hostile neighbour who dumped her products on their markets? Therefore a decade after Confederation this subsidiary motive expressed itself in a "national policy" for protecting home industries against American competition.

But prosperous though the Canadians were for a time they never ceased to hope for access to the larger markets of the United States, and in 1871 Sir John Macdonald made another attempt, but only got a free market for fish in return for the privilege of the in-shore Maritime fisheries; and in 1874 George Brown, one of the friendliest of Canadians towards the Americans, did not get much more. This era in Canada closed with the defeat of the Conservatives in 1896, Macdonald in the earlier years ruling with the fullness of his powers. On the whole the relations with the United States were not good. It was a very difficult time for Canada; the "national policy" did not bring the hoped for prosperity; depression prevailed; an almost unprecedented migration across the border of many of the finest of her people left great disappointment behind and created much misgiving as to the future; whereas in the United States there was activity, growth, and accumulation of wealth. Some thought their ills would lessen if they could only reach such purchasers. But they did not propose to come as mendicants: fisheries, canals, the St Lawrence, to say nothing of general trade, were a good *quid pro quo*. The cloud hung most darkly over the country from 1884–9, and as in its shadow men talked with one another, some found hope in a new policy called "Commercial Union," by which they meant absolute free trade between the United States and Canada—the assimilation of their tariffs, the abolition of custom houses and the division of customs revenue. At first the idea appealed to a large number of people on both sides of politics, some of the leading newspapers coming out in its favour; but by instinct the manufacturers soon turned against it and those who had already initiated transcontinental railway construction, as well as many who were afraid that dependence on Washington in tariffs might lead to political entanglements. Though it was not adopted by either party as a policy, the Liberals, who took "Unrestricted Reciprocity" as their platform, came nearer to it than the Conservatives, and they suffered defeat on the issue in 1891. This result was partly due to reaction against the United States, the McKinley Bill, which went into force in 1890, being accepted by the Canadians as almost a challenge to a trade war. One moral possession the Canadians would never traffic in—their own independence; and if Commercial Union should lead to annexation, such

economic advantages as might follow would be purchased at too high a price. Nevertheless, immediately
after the election the Conservative government again
sent a mission to Washington, but Blaine was in
control, and as might have been expected they found
the door closed.

Sir Wilfrid Laurier came into power in 1896 with
a desire to cultivate friendly relations with the United
States, but unfortunately in that year the Cleveland-
Olney message deepened the antagonisms between
the two peoples, and when McKinley succeeded
Cleveland the high protectionism of the Dingley Act
of 1897 was the only response he made to Laurier's
low tariff ideas. The Canadian budget of that year,
offering on behalf of the Dominion preferential treatment to British trade, was in a very real sense a reply
to the high tariff of the United States; though, as
Professor Dunning remarks,

no great access of hostile feeling in the United States towards
the Canadians was manifest as a result of this preference. It
was regarded by many Americans as a natural and properly
spirited response to the McKinley tariff of the preceding year.
This law administered almost fatal blows to certain important
Canadian industries, and it was accompanied by the rejection,
so peremptory as to be almost insulting, of overtures from
Canada looking to the renewal of reciprocity as in 1854[1].

Though trade is supposed to be regulated by self-

[1] W. A. Dunning, *The British Empire and the United
States*, p. 297.

interest, the constituent elements of this motive are often subtly commingled with a strain of emotion, and friendly nations find it to their interest as it is to their pleasure to have interchange of commerce with one another. England and the United States had been drawing together, and the sympathy shown by England to America in the Spanish War induced a kindlier attitude on the part of the United States to Canada. It was hoped, therefore, that a Joint High Commission in 1898 would effect better trade relations between them and settle the major dispute of the Alaska boundary. There were still the Dingleys who fought against concessions on behalf of the farmers of the border states, but a schedule was drawn up designed to promote freer trade in some agricultural products and lower duties on manufactures, which might have passed through the swirling currents of Congress had it not been for the dead weight of Alaska.

Little was heard of trade relations for some years. In this period prosperity, long delayed, came in rapidly like the rush of a Canadian spring. The West was being discovered; its immense resources were being made known; settlers were entering in large numbers; railways followed them and opened up new regions for occupation; the mines of northern Ontario gave promise of their later development; cities in eastern Canada were being built on healthy industries; and the United States began to realize that the neighbour who had so often irritated her, and whom she had sometimes wished to brush out of her way, was becoming an excellent customer.

But in 1909 another high protectionist measure, the Payne-Aldrich bill, was introduced into the American Congress, and it created an unexampled situation for Canada. By it all reciprocity agreements except that with Cuba were abrogated, and a complete change was made in American policy. Hitherto since the first commercial treaty with France in 1778 the principle had prevailed of granting special consideration only to such nations as would put the United States on the same footing as others in respect of tariff favours; now Congress adopted the European plan of creating a maximum and a minimum tariff, the maximum duties to be enforced after March 31, 1910, against all nations which discriminated unduly against the United States in their own tariff laws. That the bill was not directed against Canada was shown in the readiness of Congress to treat Canada's preference to Britain as an exception, or rather as being domestic within the Empire; but difficulty arose from the recent action of Canada in having given France by treaty minimum duties in return for concessions. The United States demanded the same terms as France had received, though she offered nothing in return and had a high tariff against Canada.

Canada refused and an economic war seemed imminent, to the disquietude of both countries, as an immense trade had grown up between them. Fortunately a President was in office, Mr Taft, friendliest of Americans to Canada, who wished to use all his powers to avert trouble, but he could not discover any preference equivalent to that which France had given to Canada to fulfil the terms of the bill, and Canada would not be forced, her old spirit of independence once more asserting itself. Not that she was ill disposed, for the government went half way in accepting a minor concession, which Mr Taft suggested, and gave the United States her scale of intermediate duties, in return for which Canada received the minimum rates authorized by the Payne law.

Successful in this, Mr Taft ventured further in an effort to bring the United States and Canada into closer relations, the first of Republicans to make such a serious attempt. Even those Canadians who refused the reciprocity he offered believe that he was prompted by a friendly spirit towards his neighbour whom he knew far better than did any of his predecessors in office. Doubtless also he believed it to be good politics, and would not have made the offer had he not been aware that for some years the atmosphere had been sensibly more genial. He knew also that the Laurier government would lend a favourable ear to his proposals, and was assured that the Canadian people were ready for freer trade. But he encountered much opposition in getting the assent of Congress, some members of which may have thought of McKinley's words in introducing his bill in 1890, "We have been beaten in every agreement of reciprocity we have ever had with any nation of the world," which, incorrect though they were as regards Canada, doubtless expressed a view that was widely held in the United States. By this bill, natural products were to be placed on a free list, or on a very low schedule of duties; as regards manufactured articles Canada was to do little more than put a limited number of them on her intermediate tariff; and no demand was made for concessions to compensate for Canada's preferential treatment of imports from Great Britain. The bill did not take the form of a treaty, but of legislation to be adopted concurrently by both legislatures. After a severe struggle a special Congress passed the bill in July 1911, and it was to go into effect as soon as the House at Ottawa took action. No such offer had ever been made to Canada, for the Reciprocity bill of 1854 was prepared for chiefly by Lord Elgin's earnest efforts. Then came the surprise. For nearly half a century both political parties in the Dominion had sought freer trade with the United States, and here was an agreement signed and sealed by a friendly President offering Canada what she had so long desired, without interfering

with the British preference or requiring much re-
duction in duties on her own manufactures. The
government of Canada also had pledged themselves
to co-operate in concurrent legislation, and were so
sure of their ground that they appealed to the country.
But by a decisive vote the people of Canada in
September 1911 refused to accept the offer of the
United States.

A variety of causes contributed to this decision,
some of which were political in the narrower sense.
Sir Wilfrid Laurier had been in power since 1896
and the pendulum was swinging against him. Another
most potent cause was the new spirit that had arisen
in Canada. The country was prosperous and the
people having won greater confidence in themselves
were unwilling to undergo the risk of subordinating
their commercial system to the humour of the
American Congress. Their experience of its proceedings in by-gone years made them hesitate to put
confidence in a continued favourable attitude to
them, for this was the first evidence of generous
sentiment. Canadians were now building up their
own industries, and they feared the dislocation of
trade and the disorder into which the country would
fall were Congress in the future to change its mind
and annul the reciprocity agreement. Railway and
transportation companies were alarmed. If with reviving prosperity new channels of trade were being

created at enormous cost, why endanger these east and
west lines by switching the volume of trade north
and south, and so empty the ports of Canada of their
ships? Eastern manufacturers believed that they
would lose their western markets, and eastern banks
the custom from the numerous branches which they
had opened on the prairies and in British Columbia.
Milling interests were disturbed, the fruit growers of
the Niagara peninsula feared competition, those interested in natural resources claimed that raw materials
would be ruthlessly seized by wealthy American
companies with which Canadians could not compete.
All this made a powerful argument to present to a
people who had slowly acquired a sense of nationhood. Was Canada to become economically subject
to the United States? Behind this lay an appre-
hension that reciprocity might lead to political sub-
ordination, and this developed into alarm when
Mr Taft himself said "Canada is at the parting of
the ways," and by this legislation she would become
"a mere adjunct of the United States." In many
minds the alarm grew quickly into a foreboding at
the words of Champ Clark, Speaker of the House,
"I am for the Bill because I hope to see the day when
the American flag will float on every square foot of
the British North American possessions clear to the
North Pole."

The Americans were surprised but they took the

reply of Canada calmly; indeed, it seems to have awakened in them more regard for a neighbour whom they had not yet fully understood. Years before they themselves had used the same arguments against those who advocated free trade between them and Britain. If Canada, having become mistress of her own household, would make no move that would threaten her economic independence, that was her own affair; and they could not refrain from respecting her when for the sake of preserving the ideal of her nationhood she could sacrifice what seemed to them to be her immediate material advantage.

Now that the clouds of partizan strife have drifted far off the question is sometimes asked whether the fears of those who rejected Reciprocity were well founded. A dispassionate answer, however, cannot be given, because the intrusion of the War has dislocated many factors that entered into the situation. Moreover, the continuance or decline of prosperity on one or both sides of the line would have been a ruling element in the case. It is, therefore, more reasonable to consider trade relations as they exist to-day, and to endeavour to outline prevailing tendencies.

The War introduced unprecedented conditions into Canada, among which not the least influential on her trade has been the self-confidence created by the conduct of her people at home and in the field.

It proved that they possessed organizing ability of a high order and that the skill of her expert technicians was equal to that of her neighbour. But in addition, vast amounts of new capital were brought into the country during those years by the expansion of her general trade and the specific manufacture of munitions. Financially she has become a new country. Her national wealth was estimated by the Dominion Statistician in 1919 at sixteen billions of dollars, a remarkable increase from two billions in 1911; and though the War cost her over two billions it is probable that the loss has been made good through the immense development in manufactures and food production which it stimulated. Canadians hold eighty per cent. of their own debt, they have made large investments in publicly owned undertakings, and they exhibited their resources in 1923 by rapidly absorbing a government loan of two hundred millions of dollars.

The amount of outside capital invested in Canada has risen from four hundred and fifty million dollars in 1890 to over four billion, six hundred and forty million dollars at the present time, but simultaneously the United States has been displacing Great Britain from her position as an investor in the country. In 1900 by far the greater part of the invested capital was British; now American investment is at least equal to if not larger than that from Great Britain.

Of the total investments in manufacturing industries fifty-eight per cent. are owned by Canadians, ten per cent. by residents of the United Kingdom and thirty-one per cent. by Americans, these last valued at eight hundred and fifty million dollars. One-fourth of all the foreign investments of the United States are in Canada, which has now become the most attractive of all countries for the American who has money to send abroad. This investment brings with it the industries which it supports, and with the industries come the managers and expert staffs, who naturally introduce into these branches the methods of business of their head offices.

In transportation Canada has been very directly influenced by the United States, as also in general communication services, the mails of the two countries being forwarded as though they were parts of one nation. Across Ontario the Michigan Central Railway has a connecting link for its system between east and west; and through New England, Michigan and some of the north-western States there run lines which belong to the two great Canadian systems. Railway equipment, traffic organization and management are so nearly uniform in both countries that men trained on American railways are often transferred to Canadian lines, the two most conspicuous examples being Sir William Van Horne and Lord Shaughnessey; and American influence as to wages and freight rates is reflected at once north of the border.

Canada has become a great exporting nation. Though her population is small she stands fourth in the world in the volume of her exports and first in the *per capita* value of her foreign trade. Until the War four-fifths of this trade was with Britain and the United States, the former buying from Canada, the latter selling to her. But since the War the ratio has been rapidly changing. In the year ending March 31, 1924, Canada exported products to the United States valued at four hundred and thirty million dollars, or forty-one per cent. of the total trade; and at three hundred and sixty million dollars, or thirty-four per cent. to Great Britain. To the United States went timber, paper, pulp, farm and animal products, furs, fish, nickel, gold and other minerals; to Great Britain went wheat, farm and animal products in larger proportion. The imports into Canada from the United States, constituting two-thirds of the whole, for the same period were valued at six hundred and one million dollars as compared with one hundred and fifty-three million dollars from Great Britain. Of the former far the largest item was coal, after which came petroleum and raw cotton, together with a great variety of manufactured articles, finished or in parts. However, Canada is fortunate in her vast water-powers, which already have been developed on an extensive scale and will increasingly make her less dependent for fuel upon her neighbour, while in the West and in Nova Scotia her coal-fields are of almost limitless extent.

As we have seen, the United States takes from Canada more than any other country, and Canada is her second-best customer. So close, in fact, is the relation in trade between these two countries, that a recent commerce report of the United States Department of Commerce (November 3, 1924) states:

Economically and socially Canada may be considered as a northern extension of the United States, and our trade with Canada is in many respects more like domestic trade than our foreign trade with other countries. The movement of industrial raw materials from Canada into the United States and the return flow of a miscellaneous assortment of partly or wholly manufactured goods is not unlike a similar flow between the west and south, and the more industrialized north-eastern part of the United States.

The first words of this quotation would not be accepted by a Canadian as expressing the truth, for the American continues to exclude his neighbour as far as he may from his markets by an ever-rising tariff. The American farmer is afraid of his neighbour's wheat, other field products and cattle; and no wonder, for in the Chicago contests the Canadian has more than held his own for quality of production; but the American miller must get the wheat because it is required to make the best American flour. The price, however, is now determined by the world at large and he must compete for Canadian grain as those from other countries do. The rapidly growing centres of industry in the United States with aggregations of population will, before long, take increasing quantities of food from Canada; they now absorb Canadian paper, pulp, lumber, furs, fish, asbestos and nickel, and in time much of these exports will take the form of manufactured or semi-manufactured materials. The Dominion is no longer a series of depressed provinces bargaining for markets with a powerful neighbour, but has become a world trader; and the American, ever quick to recognize material success, is realizing that he must accept the Canadian as a worthy rival in the world's commerce.

Notwithstanding this rapid growth in production and in wealth, mutterings of alarm have quite recently been heard in some eastern manufacturing centres lest the American is getting such a grip upon the Dominion that in a few decades by means of peaceful penetration Canada will be Americanized. This is merely another form of the old cry of Goldwin Smith as to manifest destiny. Even those Americans who under protection have established branch institutions in Canada have nothing to gain by annexation.

In considering economic relations between these two countries, several facts must be borne in mind. The most acute problems of Canada to-day arise from

the different needs of the widely separated parts of
the Dominion. Ontario and Quebec are not merely
great agricultural provinces but have become highly
industrialized. The cities and towns depend upon
manufacturing, and their ambitions lead them to
expect stabilization and extension of present conditions. But manufacturers are excluded from the
American markets for most of their finished products
and therefore they wish to retain the trade of the
whole Dominion. Even if they had free access to the
United States they might be at a disadvantage owing
to their distance from the coal-fields, though Canadian
goods are winning their way in the wider markets of
the world. Therefore they will continue to demand
a protective tariff, and in this they will be supported
by the great railway systems and by governments
which have to finance the national debt. On the
other hand both the Maritime provinces and the
West would like freer access to the United States in
order to sell and purchase in the larger and nearer
market. There is much restlessness in these sections
of the Dominion, partly due to a feeling that Ontario
and Quebec are treating them unfairly, partly also to
geographical situations difficult to ameliorate. To
resolve these divergent interests constitutes one of
the greatest problems for Canadian statesmanship.
Whether even with growing friendliness and also the
desire to get a share of the developing wealth of the

Dominion the United States will make any offer such as the manufacturing centres would accept and as would meet the demands of East and West is very doubtful. It may, however, be assumed with confidence that the Dominion will hold together and her economic policies be shaped to suit the will of her people; also that she will become more capable of holding her own in competition.

The standard of living of the average man in the United States has risen very rapidly by reason of the great prosperity of the War period and the succeeding years, and it is very difficult for the Canadian to keep up with the pace of his neighbour. In this respect evil communications are corrupting good manners; but it may be that the Canadian will find it necessary to live more simply and to be content with less. He has much heavier war taxation to bear and much less accumulated wealth to invest. His problem is to afford a reasonably comfortable living at home for those who will not abandon their inheritance unless the economic sacrifice involved in remaining proves too great.

Another fact is obvious to any person who knows his country's history: it has gone through two periods of much worse depression than exists at present. There is really no comparison between 1924 and 1849 or even the eighties; but in those years the people would not give ear to the charmers who wished to lead them to the rich pastures of the South; and there is no reason to think that they would do so now. The common people of the provinces have always acted on their deepest instincts of loyalty to their own country as part of the Empire; these political convictions go very deep, and Canadian individuality is a more real power than ever. Acquainted with their own past and reassured by what they accomplished during the War, most Canadians believe that the character of the people, the resources of the country and a growing immigration ensure a brighter future.

CHAPTER VI

The World of the Average Man

IT is often said that the people of the new world are simply another branch of the old in a new environment. But this is only partially so. Men and women react to their surroundings, to the vast spaces, virgin forests, untilled lands, cold winters and bright skies. North America presents geographical conditions so very different from those of Britain and western Europe that after the lapse of some generations they were certain to produce differentiation between the descendants of the same stock in the home lands and in America. As regards the United States and Canada, however, there is great similarity in respect of physical environment, and the social customs and manner of life which result so largely therefrom approximate closely in the two peoples. Both the Americans and the Canadians who constitute the kernel of their respective nations were originally for the most part tillers of the soil, clearers of the forest, and many of them adventurers on the frontier. From the beginning until recent years there has been a frontier line, though now the mysterious beyond has vanished.

Pioneers of New England and the other colonies,

some of them gentle folk, had to fight the elements from the moment of their arrival, but before many generations went by, they created a wealthy land, and from this struggle issued virtues which have been reproduced in their descendants who kept moving out into the unknown regions of the West. This most enduring and vigorous stratum in the life of the American people can be traced from the East through to the West, like a belt of rich soil. Containing different elements also from the southern and middle Atlantic states it became in the central states a new source of idealism, which to-day still underlies all the superficial materialism of those prosperous commonwealths.

To understand the American it is necessary to know what manner of man the old Puritan was. He was most tenacious of his purpose, and to him mainly is due the victory of the English tongue and of Anglo-Saxon civilization in North America. When he arrived the French were getting a foothold in Canada, and the Dutch on the Hudson, but New England with its 26,000 settlers soon outdistanced both and moved steadily into the South and West. In the spirit of the old Athenians some Americans have grown tired of hearing the praise of the Puritan, and they have been at pains to paint him harsh and repellent, and doubtless with some truth; but no part of America has produced sturdier patriotism, more original character and more genuine literature than the old puritan homeland. And so far no other single strain has been able to prevail over it in the country. The puritan's character, rooted in faith, resulted in a strange paradox. He believed that the world could bring him no abiding comfort; he scorned it as the instrument of the Devil, but in his masterful disdain for this foe he proved that he could beat him at his own game, and he filled his pockets with his winnings. He was no pacifist. Believing in an eternal opposition between the flesh and the spirit, the world and the Kingdom of God, he cried, "Up and Smite! By the spirit of the living God ye shall prevail." This was the stuff out of which excellent pioneers were made and its quality was enduring.

The intense idealism of early New England had waned before the valleys of the Ohio and the Mississippi were settled, but it received new strength when the slavery issue sundered people again according to origins and innate moral standards. Springfield, Illinois, became the home of Lincoln, where also he lies buried, and to this day it is with good reason a Mecca for Americans, for in the valleys of the great central rivers are to be found in largest numbers the descendants of the puritan East, who in Illinois, Iowa and Kansas cling with almost aggressive conviction like their forefathers to their republican democracy as being the final manifestation of political idealism.

Strong as this puritan element has been in the United States, it has hardly entered into Canadian life. Few loyalists were of that stock, fewer still of the later settlers, and the original New Englanders of Nova Scotia can hardly be said to have contributed a distinctive strain to the national character. But in so far as Puritanism denotes an attitude towards life, an ethical temper characterized by restraint and based upon religious conviction, it is one of the qualities of the Canadian people, whether French or English-speaking. The French *habitant* is a Catholic puritan, the average English-speaking Canadian a Protestant puritan, both of them tending to the severe, to simple preceptual conduct based on Divine sanctions, and avoiding sensuous and unrestrained emotion. But the derivation of this idealism is in the one case from the peasants and fisher-folk of Brittany and Normandy, and in the other from the rigid Protestantism of Scotland, the North of Ireland, English non-conformity and a section of Anglicanism.

Puritan influence has however been only one factor in the formation of the more recent American character. All sorts and conditions of men moved into the opening spaces of the West—religious and irreligious, adventurers and dreamers, materialists and idealists. Many having thrown off the restraints of their eastern homes were impatient of law and order.

Strong-willed men took the lead, and if they were coarse, as circumstances often helped to make them, they coarsened communities. Force, cunning, shrewdness were quite as common as virtues, and in the swirl of passions idealism was often submerged. The frontier man was full of adventure, he carved his home out of the rough for himself by his own energy, and took rank by the ability he showed in subduing conditions. Therefore individuality, reluctance to acknowledge a leader, and equality in social life were notes of the new democracy. Most, however, were content to seek a comfortable home in which they could transmit to their families the older institutions of the East adapted to the new environment. Some had a vision of a new earth that was to be established in righteousness beyond the mountains. Sects jostled one another for place, revivals and excitement under denunciatory preaching were common, and asceticism became the easy rule for such earlier and cruder stages of the religious life. Hard doctrines were flung at men who were accustomed to meet hardship in nature and too often in their neighbours[1]. Their life was lonely and monotonous; it had little beauty, and such as it had was clear cut, not subtle and charming. Plain fact, not poetry, appealed to them. But above all, with faith in their creative power

[1] See F. M. Davenport, *Primitive Traits in Religious Revivals* (1905), p. 63.

they made boast of their freedom; they were self-sufficient and revolted against the culture of the East. A note of the fantastic often appeared in their theories of religion, conduct and economics. Fluctuations in crops and in the prices of farm products induced the agriculturist to turn in times of depression to impossible solutions which took shape, for example, in the populist movement of the western states in 1892, and in the demand for venturesome remedies in 1923 when the farmer vented his indignation on railway corporations and bankers on finding that, partly because of his own over-capitalization of his land, he could not make his wheat pay. He knew little or nothing about world markets. The influence of the frontier is thus described by Professor Turner:

To the frontier the American intellect owes its striking characteristics. That coarseness and strength combined with acuteness and inquisitiveness; that practical inventive turn of mind, quick to find expedients; that masterful grasp of material things, lacking in the artistic but powerful to effect great ends; that restless, nervous energy; that dominant individualism, working for good and for evil, and withal that buoyancy and exuberance which comes with freedom—these are the traits of the frontier[1].

The western states have passed the first stage of settlement and have already a character of their own, in which the frontier qualities are being toned down

[1] F. J. Turner, *The Frontier in American History*, p. 37.

or are disappearing. But even on the prairies the old American is essentially conservative, and the community has fashioned the individual more powerfully after its own ways of thinking and acting than is the case in western Europe. Its "Main Street" is less interesting than the "High Street" of Britain; there are fewer characters in it, fewer than in rural New England. The unbroken settlements of well-to-do multitudes on the plains give them a sense of power, and they profess no fear of their democracy, but under its guise a section of people not infrequently becomes tyrannical, especially in times of stress and strain, when turning their own prejudices into a standard of patriotism they brand as disloyal those who will not swear in terms of their own oaths. On the whole there is less freedom of speech in America, east or west, than in Britain; in the East this may be due to the innate timidity of the propertied classes, in the West to the fear lest the principles of society are not so strongly rooted as to be able to resist the convulsive shock of new ideas should they gather volume. Nor is there yet the serenity that accompanies the inheritance of ancient tradition and of firm national character.

The people of the newer states, and also of the older agricultural sections further east, have a provincial mind. They may know the geography of their own state, possibly even of their own country, but of little beyond, and having been successful in subduing nature, being emotional and buoyed up by a bright climate, they have never had to test the limitations of their mental powers. They have created a democracy which is prepared for any kind of experiment. They are further advanced in material comfort than in intellectual discipline. But with all these limitations the American of the central states is to-day not only the most representative man in the nation but also the most vital and controlling.

A challenge has been made to the supremacy of the old American during the past generation by the in-pouring like a flood of European immigration. Most of these people have come from southern and south-eastern Europe, escaping, as they hoped, to a land of freedom, and they have become, superficially at least, enthusiastic Americans, though not a few claim the right to assert their newly acquired liberty by continuing to practise their own manner of life. Hitherto ordered society has been based upon the Anglo-Saxon conceptions of the common law, arising out of judgments due to the moral quality of the stock, but the new-comers with their different ideals may in time dilute the source and fountain of legal decisions. The political machine also is undergoing a change in control; so we hear the demand for "one hundred per cent. Americanism," and for the repression of such freedom of speech as would damage the ideals which have been held to be the foundation of Americanism. Naturally the educated foreigner does not take this without protest. Having been invited to this new land he wishes to continue his own way of life, and will not cramp his characteristics into a new mould in a land of freedom. But the old American is in earnest, one evidence of which is the enactment in 1924 of a new immigration law with proportionate quotas for each nation to prevent further change in the racial composition of the population. Another symptom of this conflict of ideals is seen in the resurgence of the Ku Klux Klan movement in the middle western states, which thoughtful Americans view with no little concern. Its features are so well known that it is unnecessary to do more than briefly outline them. Originating in the southern states after the Civil war, to resist the use of the negro vote by unprincipled politicians, this secret organization has reappeared with its terrorism in the states of the middle west, and a visitor will be told at a gathering of well-to-do citizens in any of the cities that before him there are certainly a number of adherents of the order. Its power is due partly to the people having lost faith in their politicians; the machine is beyond their control, law is broken, they feel themselves isolated and betrayed; so they call up their old pioneering instincts, take the law into their own hands and in a rough and ready way mete out decisions according to the prevailing sentiment of the community in respect of good citizenship. It has been called "an organization of one's prejudices," in the South in opposition to the Negro, and even in the North as the white workman is now finding the coloured man from the south an insolent competitor; in the cities in hostility to the Jew, and in rural parts of the middle west to the Roman Catholic, especially when the occasional use of political power by some ecclesiastic, and the insistent demand for separate schools arouse the old religious antagonism.

The newer America is therefore a land of contrasts —individual initiative and public opinion shaping towards uniformity; a buoyant confidence in the success of democracy, and a subconscious feeling that it is not yet secure enough to tolerate severe criticism or revolt. The country has grown so rapidly, changes are so swift and some of the elements are so new that it is not yet certain of itself. It has still to make its calling and election sure.

The democracy of the Canadian farmer, artizan, smaller tradesman and villager is built upon foundations remarkably like those of the American. The people look upon similar landscapes, practise similar social customs, adopt similar standards of dress and have a similar background out of which their moral ideals come. Unlike the European farmer, the Canadian owns his land and has the assurance that property brings. The artizan is conscious that by his skill and energy he may win for himself the highest position, and with this latent knowledge of the *carrière ouverte aux talents* he feels himself less dependent upon the trade unions than his English brother. He also believes in the potency of the common school which he measures by the success of his neighbours.

The same frontier spirit of independence as appeared in American life is shown in the history of the English provinces. The settlers of old Ontario and the Maritime provinces were not long in asserting themselves and claiming from the Home authorities their share of government, though they received little direct influence to this end from across the border. Strange though it may seem to an American their connection with the British Empire has probably made Canadians less narrowly provincial than those of the same class in the United States. Undoubtedly they have not much to boast of in this respect. Comparatively few newspaper readers are interested in telegraphic news from abroad, or in the discussion of foreign problems. But it would seem that the Canadian does know something more of geography than the American, and for this reason: like him he has had to learn of his own country, but unlike him he has found it necessary also to become acquainted to some extent with the leading features of the life of a powerful neighbour; in addition, belonging to the British Empire he has been taught the history of the Mother-Land, and in recent years something, at least, in regard to the nations that compose the British Commonwealth. Moreover, Canada was long enough in the War to get an acquaintance with the complex world of Europe, and this generation at least will not forget that experience and will continue to have a wider interest in outside affairs.

It can hardly be denied that the Canadian is more tolerant than the American in regard to the religious convictions of his public men. During the long process of the nomination for the presidency on the Democratic ticket at New York last June, again and again it came out that one of the candidates could not be elected because he was a Roman Catholic. In Canadian politics there is nothing to correspond to such highly emotional scenes as were then enacted, but especially would a determined effort be made to avoid the introduction of the religious beliefs of any of the candidates. Whether it be from the constraint of Quebec or the larger infusion of British stock, no such question has yet arisen in Canadian federal elections. Sir John Thompson, who became premier shortly after Sir John Macdonald's death, was a devout Roman Catholic but had been brought up a Methodist, and shortly after his death Sir Wilfrid Laurier, a French Catholic, held for fifteen years the

12–2

undivided allegiance of the Liberal party, in which there was a strong Protestant element. Quebec has certainly made the Canadian face the fact that in his country there are two civilizations to be taken account of; the importance of which as differentiating his social order from that of the United States is not often realized.

The thoughtful Canadian understands and sympathizes with his American neighbour in respect of the problems raised by the incoming alien population. Similar problems are facing him, and relying as he does on the system which Lord Shaw has called "the Law of the Kinsmen," he views with alarm any weakening of the principles of common justice and any undermining of Anglo-Saxon civilization. But the Canadian knows nothing so far of self-constituted bodies for the enforcement of order. He is proud of the impartiality and the swift execution of justice within his boundaries. Moreover, he believes, as the American does not, in responsible government, and having put a party in power he has so far trusted it, and allowed his representatives to follow out their policies without demanding that they be referred to his own judgment.

In the western provinces the influence of the American of the central states has made itself more felt than in Ontario, though as we have seen the East first gave the West its ordered society and its dominant ideals. As might have been expected, the American new-comer into the prairie provinces has not yet grasped fully the meaning of responsible government. Being something of a radical he proposes more direct methods than he finds in the Dominion of Canada. Consequently on occasion, with his pioneering energy, he may suggest the Initiative, the Referendum and the Recall, though so far without much success. Accustomed to the small banks in the United States he does not understand the Canadian banking system with its head offices in the East and their branches in the West which may charge him a higher rate of interest, so he is clamorous for new methods of credit. In support of education he is at least as liberal as other members of the community, though the standards are still determined by the Canadian of British origin. He is a good member of the community, takes his part as a trustee, is a vigorous if crude speaker, delights in large conventions for grain-growers, and though inclined to fads and fancies he responds well to humanitarian appeals and makes a kind neighbour, and by his practical knowledge has done much to develop his adopted home.

The Church fulfils a large function in the life of both peoples, but in respect of this institution, as also holds in the case of higher education, the influence of the one country upon the other has been less than in practical affairs. As far back as 1835 De Tocqueville remarked, "There is no country in which the Christian religion has a greater influence on the soul of man than in America," and fifty years later Lord Bryce virtually agreed with this view when he said, "The prevalence of Evangelical Protestantism has been quite as important a factor in the intellectual life of the nation as its form of government[1]." Two such typical though very different Americans as Cleveland and McKinley exhibit profoundly religious convictions; both express their sense of duty in their public acts as an endeavour on their part to follow Divine guidance, and hold to the belief that the history of their people is being directed by a Supreme Will. Nor are these isolated cases. In American biographies and histories one finds constant confirmation of a statement of Mr J. Ford Rhodes that the belief is widespread in America "that when a man dies he must face a personal God and give an account of his actions on earth."

In the United States, Protestantism accounts for about seventy per cent. of the population, and Roman Catholicism for about sixteen per cent., the other large sections belonging to the Jewish faith and to the Greek Church. It may be said without fear of successful contradiction that it is in the Protestant Churches that the most distinctively American traits of character predominate, though the influence of the

[1] *The American Commonwealth* (1910), p. 827.

self-confidence and idealism of the new world is traceable also in other religious communities.

From the earliest days to the present the member-ship of the churches has consisted of the orderly, progressive classes, and they have been served in general by an educated ministry, many American preachers having proved themselves intellectual leaders and orators of the highest distinction. Their influence has made itself felt in varying measure in the newer parts of the country; but it must be ad-mitted that the intellectual side of Protestantism is relatively less influential throughout the United States than might have been expected. Unfortun-ately the rapid expansion of the American West more than two generations ago found the regular organiza-tions of the Churches unable to cope with the religious needs of the new communities with anything like the quality of service they had given to the older East. It was, therefore, swept by emotional and often fan-tastic appeals, which like a quick fire on thin soil destroyed here and there layers of earth in which good seed might have taken root, and its fertility can only be recovered with time[1].

A Swiss observer who has recently made a study of American Protestantism gives his book the sug-gestive title of *Dynamis*, thus interpreting its most characteristic feature as *Energy*. Just as so many of

[1] Davenport, *op. cit.* chap. x.

the American philosophers have run to pragmatism, their preachers also, easily yielding to this tendency, have eschewed basal problems of religious thought and take social and moral questions as the themes of their discourse. Standards of conduct which have secured the approbation of their community are prescribed as the garb in which religion must array herself if she is not to be an impostor. In this respect they have gone further than their nearest religious kinsfolk, the English Non-Conformists and the Scottish and Irish Presbyterians. As for the Church of England, the average American, particularly of the middle West, understands it no more than he would the aristocratic society of England, though in the larger cities and the older East an increasing number, some of them of Puritan and even Quaker origin, having grown impatient of a sermon that does not constrain them by its power, find satisfaction in the beautiful ritual, the sacramentalism, the reverence and the submissiveness of the Protestant Episcopal Church.

A disconcerting phenomenon of the religious life of the western world is the extraordinary reaction to which the name "Fundamentalism" has been given. The fundamentalist appeals to the authority of post-reformation Confessions and lives theologically in an era of arrested development. Though this attitude of mind is found in all countries, it is relatively much stronger in the United States than elsewhere.

Churches are being riven in twain and some fear a permanent cleavage in American Protestantism. The American is intensely in earnest about his religion. It is a primary source of his idealism, and whatever might imperil it he will repel with vehemence. The old doctrines worked; they must be true. They are the law of the Church; they must be obeyed as the laws of the land must be obeyed. New doctrines are bringing unrest to the outside world. He demands, therefore, for his "one hundred per cent. American-ism" a religion based upon creeds that he believes have hitherto never been overthrown, hoping that peace will result therefrom. The non-churchman would naturally wish not to be sucked into the im-petuous channels where religion and theology meet, but lately to his surprise the current has been swirling up around his schools and colleges, and he finds himself in an intolerable and almost incredible position. Led by Mr W. J. Bryan, certain elements in some states of the south and middle West have been conducting a campaign in their legislatures, with disquieting success, to prohibit the teaching of evolution in all schools and institutions supported by the state. Quite recently a teacher in Tennessee has been arrested and indicted for having violated a statute of the legislature which forbids the dissemination in state-supported schools of a theory of evolution which "disregards, denies, or brings into disrepute" the Biblical narrative of creation. It seems probable that eventually the Supreme Court of the land may have to determine whether such action of the legislature was constitutional[1].

In a democracy also where everyone can read and write the average man considers himself a competent judge on anything that so deeply affects him as religion. Experts are relatively fewer than in lands with an older civilization, and they are listened to with less respect. A blind leader, therefore, may in times of unrest lead multitudes of sincere, panic-stricken followers into a ditch. But the American democracy will, it is to be hoped, gradually take to itself more reasonable and clear-sighted guides, as those going out from the universities and colleges have been set in the way of doing some thinking for themselves, and are being equipped to estimate what is intellectually fundamental in the spiritual life.

On passing to Canada the visitor will find himself in a different religious atmosphere. The prevailing breezes come from different quarters, and centres of high or low pressure do not move, as on the charts

---

[1] Since the delivery of this lecture the attention of the world has been directed to the trial in Tennessee, in which the two sides have been brought into open conflict before a tribunal pathetically incompetent to decide the issue. The dramatic death of Mr W. J. Bryan is by no means the close of the chapter, which cannot be finally concluded by any court of law.

which forecast the weather, from south of the Great Lakes into the North and East. In Quebec he will discover, as we have seen, a devout and very conservative people, whose leaders have no sympathy with the Americanized views of the Roman hierarchy on the other side of the border. These leaders have in the French language a fortress into which they withdraw their flocks when Modernism in morals or beliefs sends even a few of its scouts to scan the peaceful valleys.

Of the total population of Canada nearly fifty-seven per cent. is Protestant in religion, and over thirty-eight per cent. Roman Catholic, of the latter nearly one quarter being non-French including several hundred thousand newcomers from central or southern Europe.

Modern Canadian Protestantism is not closely associated with that of the United States, though in its origin it could not escape the influence of its old home. Some Anglican clergymen came over with the loyalists, and not a few Presbyterian churches retained connection with the original Synod in New York state, but after the War of 1812 this relationship was almost entirely dissolved. Most American influence, however, entered with Methodist preachers from the United States who were active in establishing congregations among the settlers in Upper Canada, and who for more than a generation passed to and fro across the border. When immigration set in from Britain the churches in the Old Land were so slow in supplying the spiritual needs of those who had left, that for a time in some sections communities were in danger of moral deterioration; but the situation was saved by the devoted service of missionaries of great earnestness and character whose work is traceable to this day in the fields in which they laboured. As the decades went by the two missionary societies of the Church of England, those of the Scottish Churches and of the English Methodist Churches took deepening interest in the colonies, and the connections were firmly established which have been maintained ever since. A quarter of a century ago in Ontario there was many a small village or town which might almost have been transferred from sections of England where Non-Conformity is strong, or from the southern counties of Scotland; and not a few country sections of Ontario and the Maritime provinces were little more than Highland parishes in the new world.

The Church of England, the Presbyterian Church and the Methodist Church are to-day about equal in numbers, and the relative strength of the Anglican Church in Canada as compared with its position in the United States has been an important factor in differentiating Canadian nationality. Her tradition and her dignity have steadied the mind and repelled

extravagances. The Presbyterian insistence upon an
educated ministry has created a high intelligence and
has restrained emotion, and the Methodists, while
retaining their evangelical fervour have come to dislike exuberant expression[1]. Taking to heart the
experience of the United States, and exhibiting the
missionary spirit of their founders, the Churches of
Canada sent in strong men to accompany the settler
when he entered the Canadian West, with the result
that that portion of the country never got out of hand.
The Churches are like bands, holding together all
the provinces[2].

The important fact is that these three largest
Churches have been reinforced from Britain, and
the theological views that have prevailed there have
been transferred to Canada; one result of which
has been that though fundamentalism has entered
into a few Canadian circles by way of the United
States, it has not made headway comparable to
its growth south of the border. It has often been
remarked that Canadians are less emotional and more
reflective than Americans, and that they will listen
with more sustained attention and have not to be

---

[1] Cf. Davenport, *op. cit.* pp. 299 f.

[2] Since the delivery of this lecture a union of the Congre-
gational, Methodist and Presbyterian Churches of Canada
has been consummated. This unique accomplishment is due
entirely to Canadian conditions and was in no way the result
of American influence.

humoured to the same extent in public addresses. Possibly this accounts largely for the fact that the people have not been subject to such passions of revivalism, nor have been so much perturbed by theological controversy. An eminent Frenchman has said that "the Americanization of Canada is retarded by the distinctly British complexion of Canadian Protestantism"; and it is interesting to note that another recent French visitor has been impressed by the British element in the religion of the Dominion: "On dirait que l'armature morale qui maintient la solidarité des gens de la ville ou du pays est faite avant tout de ces traditions religieuses; tout changera autour d'elles; mais elles seront conservées[1]."

The Common School has been from early days one of the most powerful influences for the moulding of the character of the American people, among whom there is a deeply rooted and well-nigh universal conviction that the freedom of their democracy depends upon their education. In fact, the genuine American rivals the Scot in his determination that the advantages of the school shall be placed within reach of all classes of the community. As far back as 1790 laws were in force in all the northern states making provision for the instruction of children in the rudiments of knowledge, and in New England nearly every

[1] M. Jaray, *Revue des Sciences Politiques*, Oct.-Dec. 1923, p. 525.

person had received a common school education. The census of that year states that every Massachusetts town of fifty householders or more was required to support a school-master to teach the children reading and writing, and every town of one hundred house-holders a grammar-school. These traditions have persisted so effectively that in the settlements of the central or middle western states that are of substantially eastern origin there has been a low proportion of illiteracy. This thoroughly democratic view both of the good of education for the common man and of its necessity as a pillar for government of and by the people, is distinctly American in the sense that it has existed as a political axiom since the birth of the nation.

The new world has never known such distinctions in educational opportunity as have prevailed in England, and this is a fundamental difference between the two peoples, traceable in American character. Not even did the loyalists who came to Canada regard education in the same light as the English aristocracy. As Americans they had known the common school for everybody, and in their new home they asked for it again. And since there were not enough teachers from Britain and among themselves to supply their schools, they took Americans, even if they were sometimes no better than vagrants, running the risks of such unhealthy political doctrines as might thereby be infused into the communities. In the early days the irregular and unlicensed teacher was a bane and suspect in all the provinces, but the people, poor and in many districts illiterate, were bound to get instruction.

The direction of education in the Canadian provinces during the first third of the nineteenth century was in the hands of men from Britain who endeavoured to establish their ideals in the new world. They thought first of universities and the grammar-schools to feed them, which were to be maintained in order that the sons of the more comfortable classes might not have to go for their education to the United States, but might be reared at home as a bulwark against republicanism. Moreover, these higher institutions, if not exclusive, were designed to serve the Anglican Church; so dissenting clergymen in self-defence championed the cause of the common people and sought to establish academies in which youths might be trained for the ranks of their ministries.

It was not until after the involved struggle for responsible government was nearly over that the common school systems began to be organized in the different provinces. The needs were the same everywhere, and fortunately men arose who understood how to meet them. At this point began the next era of American influence. The leaders of the provinces were well aware of the school system of their neighbours and they admired its success; consequently commissioners visited the United States to report upon it as it might offer valuable suggestion for the establishment of their own. In Upper Canada the man who first organized the education of the common people on the lines that it has in general maintained since, was the Rev. Dr Egerton Ryerson, who was virtually Superintendent of Education from 1844 to 1876. These early words of his might have come from an American: "Education among the people is the best security of a good government and constitutional liberty: it yields a steady, unbending support to the former, and effectually protects the latter." Dr Ryerson definitely took much from the practice and organization of the schools of Massachusetts and New York, but as a Canadian who knew thoroughly the character of his own people, he adapted his borrowings to local requirements with true administrative ability. He was the first to have incorporated into the Canadian system the American plan of local taxation imposed in return for local control. While the legislature granted financial support according to definite principles, the district also was to contribute its share, and with the revenue from these combined sources the elementary schools were made free in 1871 and attendance upon them became compulsory.

Again following his neighbour's suit, Dr Ryerson

took the important step of imposing a uniform series of text-books on the schools, but for these he turned from the American to the Irish national publications. In addition to this, the organization of the educational system of Canada has many other points of resemblance to that of the United States. The province, like the state, is the final authority; only military and naval schools, and the education of the Indian, are under federal control, though limited grants for technical and agricultural education are also made from the national treasury.

There are, however, differences that arise from the political characteristics of each people. To the south the educational structure of the communities and even much fundamental school law have been embodied in the constitutions of the several states which are administered by state boards of education, either ex-officio or nominated by constituted authority. In Canada, however, quite different principle and practice prevail. All education is under the control of the legislature, provincial boards are subject to the government of the day, and the chief officers of the province are appointed by and are under the supervision of the minister of education, though some municipalities elect their own boards of education and have their own officers. As also holds, however, in the United States authority is delegated by the province itself to local areas for the performance of certain duties, which can be more satisfactorily carried out by those on the spot who are acquainted with their local needs, especially such as go beyond the prescribed minimum essentials in education. These characteristics of educational administration in local areas belong distinctively to the continent, whether in New York or Ontario, in California or Saskatchewan.

In secondary education also Canada has adopted the American system. The English grammar-school which was transmitted to New England became changed into a high public school supported by the state as part of the system for which it was responsible. It was made free to all who were fitted to enter it, and for that reason its curriculum was broadened so as to meet the requirements of others than those who were going into the professions. Thus it came in time to occupy an intermediate place or to serve as a four-years' link between the elementary school, which covered the first eight years of instruction, and the university. A boy having reached the age of fourteen years, at the end of his elementary stage, spends his next four years in the high school, and is thus supposed to be ready for the university at eighteen. This system prevails throughout Canada, though the high school curriculum may be extended to cover five, or even six, years of work. But at present all over the continent the question is being asked seriously whether sufficient educational value is received from the four years of high school work, placed as they are at the conclusion of the eight years of elementary work. The results are recognized as not being satisfactory. Pupils enter upon high school work probably two years too late; their language training is greatly handicapped thereby, and those who go on to the university at eighteen do not possess the liberal training necessary for recruits to the learned professions.

In other respects also the United States has served as a model for Canada, through her experimentation in different types of schools and in educational methods. But Canada has learned equally as much from Britain in regard to the requirements for the physical welfare of the pupils, and in the matter of adolescent and adult education. The Fisher Act, for example, has been followed with much interest in the Dominion and has set an ideal for progress in several of the provinces.

In the field of Labour contiguity and the similarity of environment have had results parallel to those in other departments of human endeavour. Very powerful influences from the United States have for a generation been moulding the methods of by far the largest part of organized Labour in the Dominion. But there have also been national modifications and decided expressions of the Canadian spirit, as well as in recent years effective contributions from Great Britain. The American Federation of Labour is a very powerful, and, on the whole, a conservative organization, its leaders having resisted the extreme movements in the field of Labour such as in their judgment would lead to the disintegration of the social fabric, and for this reason definite cleavage exists between them and the radicals who have often resorted to violence. In both countries the rank and file of Labour is loyal to the national institutions, though there have been outbreaks in each which have not only divided the general membership but have had to be repressed with force. Canadian Labour was organized on its own lines before it became affiliated with the American Labour movement, but now the Trades and Labour Congress of the Dominion works in close association with the American Federation of Labour. The local unions of the various trades are branches of continental organizations which have their headquarters in the United States, and on the whole the Canadians have been beneficiaries by this arrangement, the contributions of the Canadian trade unions to the American Labour movement in 1923 having amounted to six hundred thousand dollars, while their benefits in return were about eight hundred thousand dollars. However, there have always been strong local labour associations in Canada which have refused to identify themselves with the international bodies, and on occasion local unions in the Dominion have rejected decisions of the international headquarters. But the American Federation of Labour and the Canadian Labour movement in general have lived together in cordial relations, and prolonged strikes in the United States usually produce sympathetic unrest north of the border. At times the cry has been effectively raised that a foreign body is in control of the trade conditions in the Dominion, but this is being counteracted by the strengthening of the Canadian organizations. Americans claim that they have not attempted to exercise any pressure whatever on the nationalism of Canada, and that "in so far as political activities are concerned, the Canadian Trades and Labour Congress is as independent of the American Labour movement as the American Labour movement is independent of the Canadian Trades and Labour Congress."

Of recent years the great influx of artizans from the British Isles into the larger cities of the Dominion, where the labour unions are strong, has been changing the situation; the new members have brought their own ideas with them. As is well known, the British Labour movement, in contrast to the American, has taken to active politics, and this distinctive phase is being reproduced in Canada, where both in the Dominion House and in the provincial legislatures there are a number of labour representatives. The Canadian

Labour Congress has gone even further in the path of the British movement and has sent its representatives to the International Federation of Trades Unions in Europe, with which the American Federation of Labour, in accordance with its principles, has refused to associate itself.

So many are the departments of social activity in which American influence can be traced that only a few of the more outstanding need be mentioned. Brief reference may be made to the Clubs which have been created for the purpose of bringing together members of the business and professional communities and stimulating them to good citizenship. Usually they meet at luncheon once a week, and as they profess an altruistic purpose, such as support of some local hospital, they are often called "Service Clubs." Their primary object, however, is to create in their members an interest in one another; a spirit of almost mechanical brotherhood prevails, with, in some clubs, a weekly recital of information about various members which must be uninteresting to the average person. Though this enthusiasm for comradeship may be superficial, the net result can hardly be other than good, and these clubs may be taken as another manifestation of the loyalty to an institution which is so easily stimulated in the American democracy, as well as of the genuine friendliness that exists among average people in the United States. In being transferred to Canadian soil the general characteristics of these clubs are preserved, though modified by the local patriotism and the less emotional qualities of their members.

There is, on the other hand, in every city and large town of the Dominion an organization which has no counterpart in the United States—the Canadian Club distinctively so called, most branches being composed of men, though there are some Women's Canadian Clubs. They eschew partizanship, and only allow politics in the larger sense, but they offer an intelligent audience, without subsequent discussion, to any lecturer who has anything to say on current affairs, domestic or foreign. It is a compliment paid to a distinguished visitor to invite him to address the club, and a large number of the leaders of the modern world have given a message through it to the Canadian people.

Conventions for social work are international. Americans are asked to speak on Canadian platforms and Canadians to take their place on American programmes; the similar environment of both makes the experience of the one, especially the larger, of great advantage to the other. All this is greatly furthered by the wide circulation in Canada of American journals and magazines which set forth for their larger constituencies the most recent and venturesome experiments in moral reform and social welfare.

But it is the theatre, the moving-picture show and the radio which are exercising the most penetrating and subtle influence upon the social standards of Canadians. The plays and the films emanate from American sources, the plays that are presented on the Canadian stage having been chosen to suit American audiences, and the films, as well as the cuts in the illustrated papers, having been designed to please the average American constituency. Every night thousands of young Canadians listen to addresses and talks directed to the people who live in the central cities of the United States. As immigrants from Europe of precisely the same character and outlook as have made their way into the United States pour into Canada, they will, through the constant repetition of similar ideas in picture, play, illustrated paper and radio, soon be moulded into a type that will no longer be Canadian, but a product of European ideas toned to the manner of life that prevails among the people of their own origin in the American cities.

Another factor in this process is the internationalization of sport. Both peoples have the same athletic heroes whose doings are chronicled in the daily papers, though Canada still retains her own style of football, and hockey is almost a national game.

The greatest and best of all influences, however, in moulding the life of Americans and Canadians to similar issues has, of course, been the possession in common of a rich language. A crude and meagre tongue may be sufficient for the few wants, chiefly material, of barbarous tribes; but a highly developed language, precise, opulent and strong, the instrument of noble literature and glorious common history, cannot but create a consentient impulse in the minds of the several peoples who employ it, and fashion them into some similitude to one another by their common heritage of ideas and emotions. Ancient words are freighted with suggestions of struggles, failures, hopes and attainments—individual and national, moral and religious. They call heroisms to memory, they express ideals, they appeal to the noblest motives. Fortunately, also, the language and literature which these peoples possess in common were shaped and most richly charged by the genius of the race before the breach made by the Revolution. Virtues were clarified and moral and political experience took shape in the earlier epochs of British history. By instinct the Canadian grasps the meaning of the American: the greatest words convey to both at once their deepest thought.

The broad-minded English-speaking Canadian will readily grant that his country is the richer for being the inheritor of two civilizations. He realises that in Quebec there are fine fruits of the Latin mind, and that there is a delicacy in the thought and manners of their cultivated people which can only be paralleled in France; also that the common folk have kept, along with the accent of Saintonge and Normandy, something of their old style in orderliness, love of home and of country.

But the vigorous civilization is English; more than the French it will mould the future of the Dominion. And the significant fact is that this language is used by the Americans. Indeed, in the very tones and words closer racial affinities are shown between Canadians and their neighbours than exist between the people of the south of England and those of the lowlands of Scotland. Experts in philology maintain that the present accent of the average people of large portions of Ontario has been derived mainly from Americans, either loyalist or later arrivals, who came from Pennsylvania and western New York. It has always differed from that which prevails in Nova Scotia and New Brunswick, which, on their western borders, resembles the speech of New England; though it must be admitted that there is a distinctive Canadian speech and tone throughout the Dominion.

The American has, of course, also made for himself a new vocabulary, retaining not infrequently an older word that has fallen into disuse in Britain. Not seldom it is a vigorous expression adapted to newer needs, often mere slang, the language of the vagabond, such picturesque phrases as a pioneer might use, for refinements and shades of meaning do not interest his society; his native humour shapes itself in some parabolic nucleus. Then there is the deposit from the speech of immigrant foreigners who take the most direct way of making their wants known by a transliteration of their own idiom.

In most of this new language the Canadian finds much that he can adopt; phrases grow familiar to him in passing to and fro and in the press. But there is also a real difference between the two peoples. Immigration from Britain into Canada throughout the years has been so great that old English and Scottish pronunciations, methods of speech and ideas abound, and the visitor from the Old Land who comes to Canada by way of the United States often remarks that he finds himself half way home.

To sum up, it appears that the average Canadian, while adopting much from his neighbour, has through his own individuality modified what he has received, and at the same time has kept open the channels along which new power has been constantly brought from the British Isles to reinforce the ruling conceptions of his life.

CHAPTER VII

The World of Higher Education

FEW worlds were further apart in the latter half of the nineteenth century than the cultivated society of the eastern American cities and the educated circles of Toronto, Montreal, Halifax and the smaller towns of the provinces. But even during that period the Universities of the United States, true to their international character, attracted and graciously received the Canadian student in quest of learning. Courteous and hospitable, the American professor welcomed his academic colleague on terms of equality, opened to him his laboratory, and communicated unselfishly with him in the promotion of his researches, and the Canadian who sees his neighbour often and at close range will gladly confess that nowhere does he find a finer type of gentleman than in the universities, libraries, museums and scientific institutions of the United States. When a new day dawned for graduate study on the continent at Johns Hopkins University, aspirants from the provinces entered on an equal footing with others, and not a little of the newer Canadian scholarship and science is traceable to this source. Since the opening of the twentieth century a steady stream has been directed to other attractive centres also such as Harvard, Yale, Columbia and Chicago, where the young graduates with Canadian degrees are given a generous share of scholarships and are accepted for advanced work in a spirit of genuine friendliness. Nor has the hospitality ceased with the award of a doctor's degree. Positions in American colleges and universities have been opened to Canadians as to Americans, even the highest places not having been withheld from them; and this not without reason, for though the Canadian is loyal to his own home and his native culture, he is more easily adaptable than most to surroundings so similar to those which he left. The rolls of Canadian colleges contain the names of nearly six hundred former students who hold academic appointments across the line. In addition to this there are possibly four thousand five hundred graduates of Canadian institutions, or about ten per cent. of the total number, who are making their living in the United States. This is not a high percentage relative to other walks in life, but in terms of quality the actual loss to Canada has been serious. Unfortunately their own country has not been able to offer them such an attractive immediate prospect as opened before them in the South, and many have gone who still live in hope of a day when they will have opportunity to return. But this depletion of strength is on the other side a reinforcement of influences which extend the intellectual and scientific constituency of those who remain at home, for in these days science and learning are not delimited by strict national boundaries.

Though American universities have adopted into their family so many of their neighbour's academic children after they have come to maturity, they cannot be regarded as the spiritual homes from which the hearth fires were carried into the northern wilderness. In how few respects the Canadian universities may be said to derive from the American will be evident on a comparison of the rise and growth of the higher institutions of learning of both countries. Canadian universities bear the imprint of their own history; they indicate the type of character and intellect that belong to their provinces.

The American college came from England and for many generations it was little more than an offshoot in a new environment. Some of the finest sons of Cambridge emigrated and founded on the banks of the St Charles river in Massachusetts, Harvard College, "that eldest of the Seminaries which advance learning and perpetuate it to posterity throughout America[1]." The second college, that of William and Mary in Virginia, was founded by the Rev. James Blair, a graduate of Edinburgh, then a vital centre of learning, who reproduced its curriculum in the more

[1] Tablet to John Harvard, Emmanuel College, Cambridge.

genial climate of the South. Yale appeared in 1701 and repeated the studies of Harvard with increased severity. In these two colleges the leaders of New England in Church and State were trained. Princeton, Pennsylvania and King's College, New York, followed in quick succession. Hitherto the primary aim of the colleges had been to educate men for the ministry of the churches, but Pennsylvania, under the influence of Benjamin Franklin, whose ideas were amplified by its president, Dr William Smith, a graduate of Aberdeen, departed from previous ideals. It was connected with no Church and its purpose was to afford a broad education "in manners and rectitude through instruction in languages, the mother tongue and all useful branches of arts and sciences." On the outbreak of the Revolutionary War the overwhelming majority of the graduates of the colleges threw themselves into the national cause, of whom such men as John Adams, Otis, Jay, Hamilton, Jefferson, Marshall, Witherspoon, were only the most outstanding. Other colleges in the north, now of established fame, such as Brown, Williams, Dartmouth, Bowdoin and Amherst, with small revenues and staffs, though occasionally distinguished by some national figure, filled well their purpose of forming the character, on a definitely traditional type, of those who were to lead the democracy. A new spirit showed itself most distinctly in the charter of Virginia, founded by Jefferson

in 1819. Without ecclesiastical affiliation and inspired by French influence, it was intended "to form
the statesmen, legislators and judges, on whom public
prosperity and individual happiness are so much to
depend"; also to provide for education in agriculture,
manufacture and commerce.

From the beginning of the nineteenth century the
old conviction of the eastern puritan that education
and religion should go hand in hand, took active form
in the establishment of small colleges in the opening
West. Often they were at first little more than high-
schools, but they followed the stream of settlement
and enriched western New York, Ohio, Indiana,
Illinois, Iowa and distant territories. Many of them
are to-day flourishing institutions, the spirit of which
is traceable in the high purpose and intelligent character of their graduates.

The American college embodies a distinctive ideal.
It professes to afford a liberal education by means of
discipline in time-honoured subjects adapted to and
modified by modern experience, and to provide a
wholesome moral atmosphere in which the character
of undergraduates who are in residence may be
fashioned to American standards. It must be admitted that in many of these colleges the social has
displaced the religious influence, and in some the tone
is set by the sons of the wealthier classes. The contrast between the meagre equipment and frugal days

of their origin and their present amenity and opulence is at once an indication of the material prosperity of the United States and of the change of view as regards the social advantage of a college education. But the tradition of the original purpose persists, and is the same *mutatis mutandis* as was created and lives in the colleges of Oxford and Cambridge which were their exemplars.

A second line of academic development is traceable from the spirit embodied in this provision of the North West Ordinance of 1787: "That religion, morals and knowledge being necessary to good government and the happiness of mankind, schools and the means of education shall forever be encouraged." This encouragement was to be effected by grants of land from the public domain for the support of education and religion in frontier settlements. The germ of the principle is found in the seventeenth century in Massachusetts, but great extension was given to it by this ordinance, according to which the sixteenth lot in each township was to be devoted to the support of education and the twenty-ninth lot to religion, and not more than two complete townships to the establishment of a university. This has proved to be a momentous policy for the development of higher education in the newer parts of the country.

The State University now comes upon the scene.

In process of time through private benefaction several of the oldest colleges have grown into universities which in all essentials compare with the historic European centres of learning. Other new universities of the same class have been established and splendidly equipped both in East and West; but the distinctive American institution is the State University, which in many instances developed out of the land-grant colleges established through the aid of the Federal Government. Of these the oldest, as it still is the most typical, is that of Michigan. Though its origin was made possible by the Ordinance of 1787, the Michigan Act of 1817

marks the formal beginning of the public educational movement in Michigan, the birth of what may without impropriety be called the Michigan idea, because first practically developed here, namely, a system of education supported by the people for the people, crowned by the university and providing for elementary training of all grades[1].

It was further enacted that "there shall be no discrimination against trustee, president, professor, instructor or pupil on the ground of religious belief or affiliation[2]." Thus the charter of Michigan marked a point of transition from the sectarian college to the university which to-day is open on equal terms to all

[1] H. B. Hutchins, *Educational Problems in College and University*, p. 6.
[2] *Op. cit.* p. 10.

the people. Other states followed rapidly on its lines; and the vast expenditures voted by their legislatures for the equipment and annual support of their universities, together with the multitudes of students who throng their halls, are the proof of the fundamental conviction of the American people, as expressed by Webster, that "on the diffusion of education among the people rests the preservation and perpetuation of our free institutions."

The rise and growth of Canadian universities have been characteristically different from the American, until the appearance of the new universities in the western provinces. There have been in Canada three King's colleges, two of them the earliest institutions of all, which were called into being partly to provide a ministry for the Church of England, established, as it was to all intents and purposes, in the English-speaking provinces; and partly to create an educated class who would resist republican ideas. They were under the control of Anglicans, old colonial or British, who wished to keep the higher education of the country in their own hands and to use it for promoting protective loyalty. The first half of the nineteenth century therefore witnessed a two-fold process: the founding by the non-episcopal churches of schools which soon developed into colleges for providing a liberal education for their people; and the gradual secularization of the state institutions. McGill uni-

versity, which was of private origin, was at first under
Anglican direction, but it too submitted to the general
change.

As for the other universities and the classical
colleges of Quebec, they have been quite untouched
by the academic experience of the United States.
Their origin being traceable to the great ecclesiastic
Laval they have preserved in general the educational
system of the Jesuits, and in many respects are similar
to one of the two main types of higher education that
prevail in France.

Not the least striking feature in the evolution of
the Canadian colleges has been the influence of outstanding personalities. They have been for the most
part British trained, and they made it their aim to
repeat in their localities the methods and substance
of the education they had received. As we have seen,
this was also occasionally the case in the United
States, but that influence practically ceased after the
great breach; whereas in Canada it has continued to
the present through the constant recruiting of the
academic staffs by young scholars fresh from the
completion of their courses of training in the British
universities.

Briefly the history of the English-speaking Canadian
university may be outlined. King's College, Windsor,
Nova Scotia, was founded on King's College, New
York, in 1790, the first in the British possessions

after the secession of the old colonies. Its founder was Dr Inglis, formerly rector of Trinity Church, New York, and later first colonial bishop, a man of broad mind for his day, who, had he not been thwarted by the Chief Justice of the province who had secured the ear of the Archbishop of Canterbury, might have introduced into his college such a tolerant spirit, as would have given little cause for the divisive courses that have been the bane of higher education in the Maritime provinces. As an offset to King's, Dalhousie University was established by the Earl of Dalhousie in Halifax in 1820 on the model of Edinburgh, to be "open to all occupations and sects of religion, restricted to such branches only as are applicable to our present state, and having the power to expand with the growth and improvement of our society." In 1785 several "loyal adventurers" of New Brunswick having sons "whose time of life and former hopes call for an immediate attention to their education," memorialized Governor Thomas Carleton as "to the establishment in this infant province of an academy or school of liberal arts and sciences." In 1800 this academy was established at Fredericton by provincial charter as "The College of New Brunswick"; and as King's College it was the first stage of the present University of New Brunswick.

The earliest suggestion for the establishment of a university in the provinces of Canada seems to have come from Lieutenant-General John Graves Simcoe, first Lieutenant-Governor of Upper Canada. In 1797 he advised the legislature to petition the King to sanction the setting aside of a portion of the waste lands of the Crown for the establishment and support of a respectable grammar-school in each of the four districts of the upper province, and also of a college or university for the instruction of the youth in the different branches of liberal knowledge. Such a practice had, as we have seen, prevailed in the old colonies and would be familiar to the loyalists. As a result, about 550,000 acres of Crown lands were reserved for this purpose, from which came the original endowment of what is now the University of Toronto.

The figure whose activities both directly and by reaction were most central in the Canadian field till the middle of the nineteenth century was Dr John Strachan, a graduate of Aberdeen and St Andrews and afterwards first bishop of Toronto. He was possessed by the idea that the State should establish and maintain a university in the interests of the Church of England; and in 1827 he secured a rigid charter for King's College, Toronto, embodying those principles, which he held would help to counteract in Canadian youth the sentiments of disloyalty. He also induced his friend, James McGill, to leave his estate for the establishment of McGill University, which was to be under similar influences.

As a result, the Methodists and the Church of Scotland founded their own colleges, which are continued until this day, the former as Victoria College, now a constituent part of the University of Toronto, and the other, as Queen's University at Kingston, Ontario, which is no longer under denominational control. The process of the secularization of King's College was slow, but it was accomplished in 1850 when it became the University of Toronto.

Hereafter in due time by reason of financial necessities there appeared a feature unique in the higher education of this continent which is known as the federation of universities and colleges in the University of Toronto. Victoria and Trinity universities, the latter established by Bishop Strachan after the secularization of old King's College, and St Michael's College belonging to the Basilian Order, are now all, as regards arts, colleges holding equal rank and enjoying equal privileges with University College, the provincial arts college, in the University of Toronto. Old denominational feuds have disappeared from the academic arena, and so successful has the experiment been that the example of Toronto has been followed in Manitoba and in Nova Scotia.

In the three westernmost provinces of the Dominion splendidly equipped universities have come into being within the past fifteen years. They signify the energy and foresight of the people who have

occupied these lands, and though in the main their
ideals, standards and spirit are those of the East, they
have in many respects followed the constitution of the
universities of the American West.

The relation of the provincial universities of
Canada to their legislatures is different from that of
the American state institutions. Under responsible
government the prime minister and his cabinet are
in the last resort supreme in such education as is
supported by the province. In order, however, to
facilitate the working of a great university, which
requires special and continuous oversight, the government delegates its control to a board of trustees or
governors, and the legislatures vote such expenditures as they approve, usually in large grants. These
governors have not the independent authority of the
regents of American state universities, who are as a
rule appointed by the governor of the state or elected
by the people at large, and who administer indepen-
dently certain inalienable federal and state revenues
as well as the grants for maintenance and buildings
which they secure by direct approach to the legislature. In Canada the governors are veritable trustees
for the government of the day.

The university everywhere and throughout its
history has been inclined to conservatism, especially
so in its central arts faculty, which piously preserves
its own transmitted conception of a liberal education.

The idea of the American college was "to train men roundly, thoroughly and well for manly and worthy living. Their spirits were to be furnished, not their pockets filled, by a course of study and training which fell just at the right period of their lives, and by close and intimate association with others having aims similar to their own[1]." It is a great tribute to the excellence of this ideal not merely that it still flourishes in both East and West, but that the faculties of medicine and engineering in the best American universities are requiring two years of a college course as a preliminary for entrance upon the specific studies of the profession, with the aim of inspiring the student with some vision of his duties as a good citizen in a free state.

But while in avowal this college course is that of academic idealism, in substance it is too often, at least in the first year, not superior to what can be got in the best high-schools. This holds in both countries, and may be explained by history and the circumstances of society. The American college takes seriously its task of educating the democracy: it, therefore, believes that it has a duty to see that the undergraduate does his work; it holds itself also responsible in measure to the parent for either discharging the youth if unfit or indifferent, or for encouraging him to success. This task is made

[1] Nicholas Murray Butler, *Scholarship and Service*, p. 100.

harder because except in the older and larger universities of the East, most institutions, and especially the state universities, do not conduct matriculation examinations, but receive their entrants on the recommendation of the principals of accredited schools, that is to say those recognized by the university as maintaining a definite standard of equipment and instruction. This has recently led to congestion of students in the first year, so that classification for teaching purposes is difficult. Hence the necessity for provosts and deans and supervisors, whose duty it is to thin out by various tests and arrange suitable groups, at a great waste, as it appears to a Canadian, of the time of competent teachers who should be giving instruction. The process of supervision continues. Day by day the pupil has his "recitation" in which he is tested on prescribed work, and at the end of the term his results, probably supplemented by a short examination, accumulate for his "credit" in the subject, and after four years when he has the sixteen or more requisite "credits" he will be given his degree. In selecting the subjects for instruction in each year the undergraduate is usually allowed wide options, though he is supposed to give heed to the advice of his dean or supervisor and, of course, is limited by the time-table. Far less emphasis is placed by the American university on the comprehensive examination at the end of a term or academic year than in the British university. Supervision more or less careful is also kept over the health of the student, medical inspection and physical training being compulsory in most institutions. The people of the United States believe in oversight; they regard it as useful in educating an efficient democracy.

In respect of methods of instruction, the average Canadian college and university has followed its British models. So far the matriculation examination holds universally as also in the older American institutions. The people know what the word "matriculation" means, and have not yet come to think, as is so frequently the case in the newer portions of the American democracy, that the mere desire of a youth to enter a university constitutes a right to do so. They recognize diversities of gifts, and while endeavouring to supply equality of opportunity in their schools, they have accepted the principle that the competent and well prepared should not be made to suffer by reason of the diversion of the teacher's time and energy to help along those who have not the aptitude nor the qualification. Matriculation being accepted, practical judgment is to be exercised in the raising of its standards as occasion may require.

When the matriculant has been enrolled in a Canadian university he is as a rule thrown more upon his own resources than his American compeer, though he is held rigidly to certain subjects that are prescribed for him in his courses. Otherwise, however, he is given a good deal of freedom. Electives are permitted but they must be so chosen that in each year, or at least at definite steps, of the undergraduate's course he will have covered certain fundamental disciplines of study. Also the examination system has been retained; in fact perhaps it is overdone, as at the end of each year the work is passed under comprehensive review.

Until the period closed by the Civil war, the colleges of the United States presented fairly uniform and stereotyped courses for the bachelor's degree in arts, the core of which had been brought over from Britain. "In 1850 Harvard taught only Latin, Greek, one modern language, either French or German, Mathematics and bits of Philosophy, History and Economics. I say 'bits' advisedly," wrote President Eliot; "they were very small fragments of these subjects. There was not a single particle of instruction given in 1850 that was not properly described by the word 'elementary.' It was all bookwork." These methods and subjects were universal and by general testimony, as for example that of the late Andrew D. White, did not stimulate the student. With its recitations and perfunctory lessons and dull grammar, Yale, he writes in his autobiography, was little more than a school except for the presence of a few men of eminence. "There was not at that time

(1856) a professor of history, pure and simple, in any American university[1]."

At the conclusion of the Civil war a new spirit entered the university no less than the nation at large; the people began to realize their resources and power. New subjects, the expansion of the sciences and the introduction of optional courses were both the result and the cause of a great change, and the effect made itself felt in the character of the younger professors. From this time forward the coming generation of instructors turned after graduation regularly to Europe, chiefly to Germany which was then in the ascendant, and there for the first time these young men found themselves in universities based upon schools which had standards as high as many of their own colleges. The word "Science," *Wissenschaft*, took on new meaning; it implied a new method. In the laboratory or the seminar the American students learned the manner and process of investigation and how to attack the sources. Returning to their own country where wealth was rapidly accumulating, they had laboratories built under the direction of modern scientists, and they persuaded the rich to provide endowments for research. Libraries were stocked with source material and their contents were made accessible for ready use. New departments were added, old ones enlarged, and relief was given from the

[1] *Autobiography*, I, p. 255.

burden of undergraduate work to those who had
caught the vision of research. Scholarships and fellow-
ships were provided to enable promising students to
continue their studies. This reacted splendidly not
only on the undergraduate arts course but on the
professional schools. The lethargy had been thrown
off; a new life entered into the universities.

The most unique result of this movement was the
creation of the Post-Graduate School. The first and
for some years the most eminent was that of Johns
Hopkins University, established in 1876 under the
presidency of Dr Gilman, to which not only Americans
of the highest literary and scientific rank were appointed but also some of the most distinguished professors from Europe. Other universities followed
suit. This idea of the post-graduate school brought
about a renaissance in American education.

The American college had its origin in England;
the post-graduate school was inspired by Germany.
Unfortunately the British universities had been unknown to the American student for two generations,
and after the Civil war he would not desire to visit
them, nor would the Englishman have given him a
warm welcome. And yet the last half of the nineteenth century was one of the great periods of Oxford
and Cambridge, adorned, as they were, by some of the
most brilliant scientists and men of learning of the
time, and shaping students of unusual quality, many

of whom became not only scholars but statesmen of worldwide fame. Unfortunately these universities, with characteristic reserve, kept their treasures to themselves; they thought only of their own people. So the American, in any case prejudiced, passed Britain by, often spoke slightingly of her scholarship and science which he hardly knew, and went to Germany for his graduate work. And Germany shrewdly took the opportunity to prepare the academic mind of America to accept her own world-supremacy. It is unnecessary to ask why she failed so utterly in the end.

Since the Great War, however, a new era has begun in the British universities which have established degrees for post-graduate students, and it may be expected that, as these opportunities become known, a large number of excellent young Americans will turn to Britain as they once did to Germany; though of course the Americans themselves realize, as the Briton also will not be slow to admit, that Harvard and a few of the other great American universities are second to none in the world as regards the quality of their professors and the opportunities they offer for post-graduate study.

But the development of post-graduate schools in the United States has been overdone, poorly endowed and too ambitious institutions competing for students on low offers, with the result that scores of doctors of philosophy are to be found in all parts of the country who do little credit to the place that sent them forth.

The Canadian undergraduate curriculum in arts owes little to American influence. Professing to offer the substance of a liberal education, it maintains in a somewhat conservative spirit the subjects and methods which it received from Britain many years ago, though as has already been remarked, graduates of British universities and of those of the United States who have joined the teaching staffs have been constantly introducing modifications. It holds true of Canadian as of American universities that much of their instruction in the first two years belongs really to secondary education. But there is one chief feature in the Canadian faculty of arts, which it has derived from Britain, which sharply differentiates it from the American, that is to say, the provision for Honours and Pass courses. This is really selective education, the attempt being made to separate students into classes according to previous preparation and natural aptitudes. Those who take the pass course, the average students, are given in a fairly balanced and not too rigid variety of subjects the elements of a liberal education. A smaller number, the more proficient in some such field as classics, history, mathematics, the sciences, receive special attention in small classes, either in the whole or the latter years of their course; and in these they acquire more thorough method and such mastery of their subject as their maturity will allow, and they take with them a fairly disciplined mind if they go into a professional faculty, or proceed to a post-graduate school. That this type of training has been successful is shown by the welcome that is given by the best American universities to honours graduates from Canada. Furthermore the honours system, or something very like it, is now also beginning to make its way in their leading eastern universities and colleges.

If, however, the United States has had little influence upon the undergraduate arts course of Canada, she has affected through her post-graduate schools the intellectual life of the Dominion. Many a Canadian speaks with reverence of the Johns Hopkins of Gildersleeve, Silvester, and Rowland, so poor in buildings, so wealthy in men; and of the abundant hospitality given him in other universities. The post-graduate school itself has also been held up before the more ambitious Canadian institutions as a necessary complement to their present faculties, if they are to fulfil the function of a university in this new nation. The time has come when Canadians, who are unable to go abroad, should be able to enter into the new world of advanced work and investigation at home. Hitherto the Canadian professor has had too much of his energy absorbed in undergraduate routine;

henceforth as the staffs are enlarged he will more frequently be allowed the time and means to make original contributions to his subject. He has in the best of his own students some whom he may associate with himself, and in advanced study he will discover a new inspiration which will quicken his undergraduate teaching as well. It is from the American university chiefly that this health-giving influence is coming in like a refreshing breeze.

Professional education, in such of its branches as depend upon the application of the sciences, is so much a creation of the past two generations that its best standards are fairly uniform in the civilized world, though it is modified by the social customs and manners of life in each country. These are, as we have seen, so similar in the United States and Canada, that the types of professional education approximate in the two countries. In America the medical course is built on practically the same requirements as in Europe, and ends in three years of clinical instruction before the period of internship in a hospital begins. America's achievement in the past twenty years is that a few of her leading medical schools have been made the peers of any in the world. There is nothing anywhere to surpass their equipment, and their courses are based on the most exacting standards. Of many second-rate schools the best that can be said is that they are on the road to extinction, and that the regulations of the leading states will soon rule their graduates out on qualification for practice. Dentistry has been almost the creation of the United States. Engineering is provided for with unstinted outlay, and the best American engineers have executed some of the greatest triumphs of their profession that the world has known. Agriculture has also become an important faculty in a great variety of institutions, though relatively it has not made the progress of other professions nor such as might have been expected in the new world.

In her professional schools Canada has been greatly influenced by the methods, aims and equipment of her neighbour. Societies of American professional men of the highest class nearly always have Canadian members. Physicians, surgeons, dentists, engineers, know well the outstanding members of their order on both sides of the line. Methods of practice are discussed and qualifications for teaching considered in annual conferences, from which, if held in the United States, the Canadian brings back with him new ambitions for his own people, or, if in Canada, is stimulated to new hope by the visiting American.

In the professions of the Law and the Church, however, the United States and Canada stand more apart, though the Harvard Law School is becoming for Canada, as it has long been for the United States, a source and example for modern methods of legal training. Also in a few of the leading theological faculties or colleges, unsurpassed in the Protestant world for scholarship and effective purpose, there are always some post-graduate students from Canada.

As might be inferred from the similar social standards that exist in the homes from which the average American and Canadian students come, their undergraduate activities follow much the same lines in both countries. There are more students with wealth in the older eastern colleges and universities of the United States than in Canada, but for the most part a thoroughly democratic temper prevails, and on both sides of the line the majority of students assume a large share, if not all, of their own support, nor is anyone thought the less of for undertaking almost any job that will help him through. But as though, at first sight, to neutralize this democratic spirit, the American fraternity bulks large in university life. This old institution, dating from the thirties or forties of the nineteenth century, consists of secret societies, known by Greek letters, of nation-wide extent through local chapters which offer residential accommodation for a large number of their members. Notwithstanding periodic outbursts of popular disapproval in the more recent state institutions, the number of national fraternities has grown to about sixty, with two thousand active branches and over sixty thousand active members. Branches, or chapters, are established in the larger universities, except Harvard and Yale; and in most of the smaller colleges where they have been refused, entrance clubs, as a rule, take their place. In the West opposition arises against them from time to time on the ground of their exclusiveness, and anywhere the criticism may be heard that they lead to extravagance, idle habits and bad college politics. On the other hand, they have many strong supporters, as, for example, the late Andrew D. White, who believed that they served an excellent purpose for the American student, who is not so mature as the European. The ritual sets before the member ideal principles of conduct; the society affords him comradeship, guidance and responsibility, and does for him something such as is done for the English student by his college, helping him culturally for his later station in life. Especially in large, non-residential universities the fraternity, it would appear, assists the individual student, who might otherwise be lost, to find himself. Of late years supervision is exercised over the local chapters by their headquarters staff, with the result, so it is affirmed, that manners and scholarship have been greatly improved in the fraternities.

Strange to say, this distinctively American creation has been adopted in McGill and Toronto, and is now entering some other Canadian universities. These large institutions, non-residential for the most part, reproduce the conditions out of which fraternities took their origin in the United States. If all students could get accommodation in small colleges there would be no reason for the fraternity's existence, but out of large bodies of undergraduates these smaller groups of friends, drawn from all the faculties, find something in their chapter that is not otherwise provided. Few complaints have been made in Canada of low moral and intellectual living, or of selfish politics. During the War most of the chapters were closed because their members had all enlisted. As for direct American influence upon the individual, there seems to be little, though the occasional visits from officials from across the line, or of "brothers" from other fraternities, are a means of promoting friendship in student days between those who afterwards will have much influence in their respective communities.

To the more undemonstrative Canadian the enthusiastic loyalty of the American Alumni to their colleges is impressive. He admits with regret that at home there is less outward and visible sign of this grace. But he is comforted on reflecting that the American is always effusively devoted to his flag and to whatever reminds him of his country's history. College loyalty is an old characteristic of the United States. In the earliest days of Harvard, Commencement was the chief annual celebration of the colony. Festivities and intellectual exercises, like their modern counterparts, attracted people of all classes. They gathered round the college which was the bulwark of the Church and was maintained by their sacrifice. This spirit became a tradition in all the old colleges and it has been transmitted to the state universities. At the annual reunion the graduate returns, if he possibly can, to express his gratitude to his college, and in company with his old friends to rejoice in her prosperity, making profession of his faith in the type of character that she has produced. In most of the larger cities there are university clubs, unsurpassed in their appointments and exclusive in their membership. But the question is often asked whether in these corporate societies the best university ideals are promoted. Conservatism of thought, ending in intellectual stagnation, may easily make a cosy home for itself in the comfortable lounges of a club, and graduates as they get on in life often exhibit the very human frailty of idealizing their own past, and having become successful they may grow impatient of contrary opinions and of the occasional eruptive power of changing thought. Not a few of the leaders of American universities ask themselves whether they have not to pay a high price for the interest that the rich graduate takes in his college, and they deem that institution happy whose benefactors are content to endow without dictating policy.

This leads directly to the question of academic

freedom, as often misrepresented by its friends as endangered by its enemies. Even British universities asking for Parliamentary support are disturbed by what that support may involve, and poor though they may be, they esteem their spiritual freedom as greater riches than such coercive treasures as Ministries of Education might bestow. As for the United States, it is a habit with a school of writers to lament the degradation into which American universities have fallen through subservience to rich graduates and millionaire trustees, or to deplore their capitulation to political control. Probably enough facts are easily producible to make such complaints plausible. It has just been remarked, for example, that there are two sides to the story of graduate support, and within the last few years there have been instances of harsh and crude interference by politicians in state universities. The public, incompetent to judge, has been stimulated to demand of the professors in its service its own economic, political or religious orthodoxy. But the picture is distorted if such aberrations are magnified. The great private and the older state universities now have firm traditions of academic freedom, and if in some of the newer states there is still ground to be won, that simply means that the process of securing liberty is always slow. Such a large personal element enters in each case into the determination of the essence of academic freedom that generalization as to the homage that is really paid to it may be misleading; but the impartial observer who knows American universities must admit that the prevailing atmosphere is favourable to the advancement of truth by discussion. That toleration, one of the rarest and finest of human qualities, is silently wielding a stronger influence to-day than formerly in the leading universities of this continent, must be evident to anyone who reads biography and the records of the controversies of the nineteenth century.

On Canada American influence in this respect has been negligible. Such suggestions of the infringement of academic freedom as there have been, and they are very few, are traceable to universal human frailties. As yet the provincial universities have not suffered from political partizanship, their boards of governors having been allowed the full privileges of their trusteeship. Private universities and colleges that depend for support upon their own constituencies have so far been given little more than enough to meet their necessities, and as the rich have not yet undertaken to supply luxuries neither have they attempted to dictate policies.

The two outstanding features in the higher education of America are the creation of the state university and the magnificent endowments that have been made for the cause of education. Considering their range, it is a remarkable fact that so little attempt has been made to control the intellectual direction of the institutions in which these vast sums have been expended. Of all endowments the two outstanding are those created by Mr Carnegie and Mr Rockefeller. These gentlemen committed their money in trust to corporations. The trustees of the Carnegie Corporation and Foundation have undertaken the support of educational and research institutions, have spent large amounts on scientific investigation, established pensions and annuity funds for university teachers in the United States and Canada, and conducted enquiries, some of which have introduced new eras in professional education. The trustees of the Rockefeller Foundation have aimed at the promotion of education on a wide and varied scale, and on the development of public health in the United States. But with unprecedented generosity they have gone beyond their borders and have conducted investigations into disease at its source and have endeavoured to clear up unhealthy areas throughout the world from which disease spreads. They have also selected a few medical schools in Britain and in Canada to which they have made large grants for the development of scientific medicine, and in Canada at least they have at the same time refrained from qualifying the gift with advice as to its disposal. The work of these two foundations is even already a remarkable tribute to the imagination and the humanity of both founders and trustees. If America has been self-centered in her trade policy and has put a wall around herself against the outside world, Mr Carnegie and Mr Rockefeller have, in the design and the execution of their purposes, displayed an intelligent altruism that has done much to redress their country's commercialism.

The most serious task that lies before the universities of the continent is the cultivation of those who are to become the intellectual leaders of the people. Democracy as it exists in America is willing to educate the masses but is careless of the few who must be carried to a high degree of proficiency. The maintenance of the humanities is especially difficult, as also of the abstract disciplines of pure science, the processes of history and speculative thought. A tradition must be established for their transmission and a large society of receptive minds be created for their comprehension. It was to be expected that hitherto literature, the pure sciences and the fine arts should have flourished in the old eastern centres, and still the eastern professor, with the precedence he assumes as incident to his academic tradition, is inclined to despair of the humanities in the state universities and to assign to them the professions and things vocational, or, as it has been expressed, "the western university will look after the body and the eastern college will look after the soul[1]."

But Professor Sherman is right in repudiating the idea that liberal culture will continue to be localized in the East. From the vigorous and vital newer districts come and will come much of the best material for the post-graduate schools. Indifference to things intellectual is not determined by longitude; the moral earnestness which will in time issue in high quality of mind will not fail the descendants of the best American stock, wherever they happen to be. And it is, therefore, impossible to estimate the value of the state university to districts in which material well-being so easily outruns the slower and steadier gifts of the spirit and exhausts itself in banality. Soon the handful will become many thousands; and in the meantime once again the few will save a city. Moreover, even by reason of the very mass production which at present endangers quality, the democracy will in due course acquire a more widely diffused education; higher grades will come into existence; a better environment will call forth the latent genius, and a more refined native culture will appear.

It will be observed by those who know both countries that the influence of the Americans upon the Canadians is greater among the average folk who meet one another in business and read ordinary news-

[1] S. P. Sherman, *The Genius of America*, pp. 159 f.

papers, than it is in the intellectual circles and among those who devote themselves to society. There are too few rich Canadians to make much display in the centres of American wealth. As for the literary groups of America, exclusive of the university circles, they have never come into direct touch with Canada. Of course, until recently her cities were small and were regarded as too provincial to produce literature that would be worth attention. Canadians were not branded as profane; they were regarded simply as farmers on distant clearings, fishermen on wintry seas, small shopkeepers and artizans none of whom would think of approaching the precincts of the Muses. Americans turned their eyes to and wrote for their own environment, the regions of Philadelphia and New York, Boston, and of late the West in some measure. It was an intelligent but exclusive society that felt a peculiar possession in Washington Irving and Hawthorne, in Emerson, Longfellow, Parkman, Holmes, Lowell, Howells, James and Cable. Channing, Brooks and Beecher, who would have graced any company, belonged to cultivated America; and John Hay, Choate and Mr Root, though citizens of the world, were at home in New York and Washington. But that whole society knew nothing of Canada, though it cannot be said that educated Canadians knew nothing of them. Their works were read, as also they were in England, north of the border, and their fame had extended widely. Long-fellow was always popular in Canada, and so were Lowell and Whittier. Parkman, of course, had his large following. Irving, Hawthorne, Oliver Wendell Holmes, Howells, James and Cable were enjoyed, and many took Emerson as a guide. When the New York *Nation* was edited by Godkin it was accepted in Canada as a literary criterion, and the monthly magazines of the eastern states have always had a good circulation in the Dominion. Nevertheless, Canadian readers have not immersed themselves in American literature. The older generation preferred simple things in line with their puritan tone of life, and the cultivated circles had catholic tastes, many of those who lived in the capitals of the provinces and in university towns having had the advantage of a good education in England. They were therefore naturally guided in their reading by what was current there. It was Tennyson and Browning, Dickens and Thackeray, Trollope and Jane Austen, Carlyle and Ruskin that were on their tables; and in some quarters Blackwood and the English magazines. Though the number of readers was not large it was of good quality. Even until to-day among the educated classes the standard has been set by the critical English judgment.

More recently Canadians are taking interest in their own literature. Here again, as in everything else, there are the two streams, French and English

—the former showing the patriotism, the simplicity and the idealism of the old French stock, from which a few poets of fine quality have sprung, one of them, Fréchette, having been crowned by the French Academy. There are also historians who have found the story of their people a rich theme for their imagination. Recently books have appeared which belong to the soil itself, portraitures of the life of the peasant in its variety of homely experiences.

English Canadian literature appeals to a wider constituency. Haliburton, the creator of *The Clockmaker*, was in a sense the father of American humour, and he has not been without successors. More recently such poets as have won recognition have owed their inspiration to Canadian life and scenery and their form to universal classical principles. Story writers and novelists, of whom there have been not a few, have found their themes in their own homeland and have done much to interpret Canada to the English-speaking world; though unfortunately some of the best writers have had to leave Canada to make their living. It may be said with confidence that the literature of Canada, which is by no means meagre or common-place, draws its inspiration mainly from her own history, her own people and her own scenery. The same is true of promising younger groups of painters who are endeavouring to realize their ideals at home in schools which show individuality and accomplishment. In music, Canadian standards have been little influenced by the compositions of the American schools, but are indebted instead for their rapid recent development to European ideals; though especially in choral and organ music English tradition and practice have been predominant. Of course, New York, which is visited by all the leading artists of the world, has become one of the great cosmopolitan centres, and Canada is within her orbit.

In general, it may be affirmed that the United States has not been a primary source of influence on Canada in respect of literature and the fine arts; but the attractive power of the City of New York has been and will continue to be felt among the younger men of letters and of art in the Dominion, especially as with her wealth she has accumulated so much of the best work of the world, and is also the headquarters of the leading publishing houses of America.

CHAPTER VIII

Canada as Interpreter

A REVIEW of the history of the relations between
the United States and Canada affords encouragement to those who believe that a better day will come
for the world when all branches of the English-
speaking peoples work in sympathy with one another.
During the twentieth century these relations have
steadily improved. There would, indeed, be little
hope for humanity if two such neighbours as these
nations could not dwell side by side in growing
friendliness. By contrast how sad is the plight of
Europe: country set against country, race against
race, frontiers watched by suspicious guardians, en-
claves and fragments of peoples only tolerated of
necessity. But North America is comparatively happy.
Fear of force is unknown, vessels of war are not seen
on the lakes nor fortifications on the frontier, and
such rivalries as exist spring not from incompatible
racial ambitions but from legitimate trade between
two peoples of mutual affinity and respect. It has
been said that "borderers are seldom friends," and
it is but human nature not to be content with the
pleasant places in which one's lines have been cast;
but after grievances have been periodically magnified

the better sense of these peoples will come to recognize that each is by comparison at least a good
neighbour to the other.

The interdependence of Canada and the United
States economically makes for the permanence of
good will. Each needs the other. United by the
great lakes and rivers in common interests, their con-
joint control is essential to the life of both peoples.
Ontario gets her coal from Pennsylvania; the United
States relies on Canada for paper, and probably will
before long rely on her for wheat and fish. Such is
the magnitude of these common interests that statesmen seek to prevent their being endangered by the
explosions of second-rate politicians, though the form
of American government allows less power to secre-
taries of state and other leaders than is exercised by
the prime minister in Britain or in any Dominion.
Readers of President Cleveland's biography are aware
how his best intentions towards Canada were thwarted
by an opposition which almost led to deadlock. It is
therefore imperative that in both countries, bound
together as they are by common interests, a large
body of mutual understanding and good-will should
be created which lesser persons with narrow interests
cannot flout.

It is evident that Canada now holds an extraordinary position of vantage in respect to the United
States and Great Britain as compared with that of

even half a century ago. There were then recurrent troubles, as from a piece of bone left in an old wound, and when it became necessary for Britain to send plenipotentiaries to Washington to negotiate their removal, they often showed impatience with the restive colony which caused them so much inconvenience. And the United States asked even more petulantly why Britain did not put a stop to the complaints of these unreasonable and ill-conditioned folk by handing them over to her. For the one Canada was not much more than a ward; for the other a child who would go into decline if left to herself. So far from being a unifying influence between the two peoples, she was in those days a source of irritation.

But now all that is changed. England regards Canada with the pride of a first-born; in the Empire she holds the prestige of age and position. The United States no longer looks upon her as an intruding colony on the continent, but respects her as a nation within the British Commonwealth and as a neighbour who will take her own way to success. The Dominion, therefore, may now play a new part. No longer thought of as factious she may become an interpreter. As for the Briton, he is gratified at the individuality of both French- and English-speaking Canadians who have worked out their character in their environment; he is quietly pleased with the new footing that his kinsmen have got on the continent from which he was almost driven one hundred and fifty years ago; he was deeply moved by the response and accomplishment of the Canadians in the War. Therefore he will listen with indulgence to what they have to say.

Canada's success also has been a powerful motive in changing the attitude of the American. He recognizes that the Canadian people have displayed no small political capacity. Discordant notes arise, it is true, from different provinces of the Dominion, many of them, however, to be silenced by prosperity, but the national life speaks to-day with a fuller and clearer voice than ever. These people have also built a commercial and social structure no less impressive than the political. The development of transcontinental railways, the strength and flexibility of the banking system, the magnitude of hydro-electric construction, the financing of the War and the organization of industry during that period have proved their practical efficiency. Moreover their general well-being, orderliness of life and freedom from crime even in the newest parts are signs of high civilization. And this result—political, commerical, moral—has been accomplished by the Canadian not as an imitator nor under tutelage; he has been the architect of his own fortunes.

Such *rapprochement* between Briton and American

as Canada may be privileged to further, will be the easier because of the change that has taken place in both peoples during the last generation. The world of America as Dickens caricatured it and of England as Henry Adams recoiled from it in the 'sixties have disappeared. Long before the War the Briton discovered that he had closer affinities with the United States than with any country of Europe; and the older American has come to see that human society and the civilization which he treasures are not as safe as he had believed. The time, therefore, is ripe.

But her function as interpreter Canada will perform not of set purpose. In fact the average man would be surprised to think of his country in this rôle. In so far as she plays such a part it will be simply by being true to herself and by living her own life where she is. When the Englishman travels in the Dominion he finds much that is strange to him in the manner of life, the conventions of society, even in the tone of speech and words. But he accepts the new world for the most part without adverse criticism, or at least regards it with an indulgent eye, as being chiefly the product of his own kith and kin. He experiences something of the process of Americanization in the larger sense, and is being so inoculated with the spirit of the continent that, when he crosses the border into the United States, he will be immune from much discomfort which otherwise he would have felt.

Having become accustomed to life in Canada he will be more tolerant of similar manners and methods as they exist in the United States; and his approach to the American being thus made the easier he will find that beneath an exterior, which had he encountered it first among aliens might have repelled him, there is a fund of Anglo-Saxon conviction and idealism which he entirely understands.

But even more important is the function Canada may perform in interpreting to the United States the character of the British Commonwealth. Americans, however, often say that they find Canadians very critically disposed towards them. In fact the remark has been made that while they welcome Canadians and grant them full privileges as citizens, they are treated as aliens when they come to the Dominion. The case of the Scotsman in England and of the Englishman in Scotland is a parallel instance, and perhaps for a similar reason. In both a smaller people has felt its nationality endangered by a more powerful neighbour. Especially in Ontario and Quebec does this state of mind prevail, where the memories of the war of 1812 and the threats made at the time of the Civil war still linger, the cooling embers being occasionally stirred anew by talk of the manifest destiny of annexation. Of late there has been perhaps less cordiality than usual, because the Canadian with his heavy burden of taxation sees such large numbers of his own people being drawn away by the prosperity of the United States. Nor has he proved his neighbourliness in facilitating the enforcement of American prohibition and immigration laws. But this situation will probably improve. Nationally each people is now assured of itself and the lines of future development are laid. As governments go, theirs are on much better terms with each other than is usual in most border countries. As for average individuals, they get on together very well indeed.

The American has received hospitably the Canadians who have come to him and has discovered them to be the most assimilable of all new arrivals. At present he is going through an experience that makes him look for allies as he earnestly endeavours to conserve his Anglo-Saxon civilization, and to none can he turn for more reliable support than to Canadians. If therefore they are veritably his best friends, will he not ask about this British Commonwealth to which they are so unalterably devoted? And when the American turns to Britain as interpreted to him by the Canadian, no longer does he discover the England of the middle of the nineteenth century, but a Britain co-operating with and leading young nations in a Commonwealth. Canada has changed from a few scattered provinces into a closely knit body functioning as a member of this larger organism. Henry Adams says that in his boyhood every Bostonian,

despite political antagonisms, was English in sympathies and feelings. The Canadian, never having
experienced any breach with the old land and being
surrounded by fresh arrivals, also turns by instinct
with deepest regard to Britain as possessing the
Throne and the Mother of parliaments, and as being
the purest source of the ideals that hold the Commonwealth together. And through this devotion the
American may be led to understand something of
the quality of the British people who inspire it.

National policies when once accepted by a people
are not easily overthrown, as is evident from the
conviction held tenaciously by the American people
that they must avoid entangling alliances. But this
fact is full of promise. What has been done can be
done. It is therefore not beyond hope that again the
American people may attain another fixed purpose,
that of sympathetic co-operation with the British
Commonwealth. That it will involve mutual forbearance is obvious, but this is necessary even between the several Dominions and the Motherland,
and also between the several sections of the United
States. Such a set purpose would serve to modify
policies which, if they were determined by one people
alone with a view to their sole interests, might cause
friction with the other. It is therefore both reasonable
and right that leaders of both peoples and men of
good-will should do all in their power to promote a

spirit of friendliness, remaining none the less true to the ideals and aspirations of their own country.

The greatest forces work silently. No hurricane or earthquake is to be compared in might and permanence with the power that binds the surface of the earth in winter or loosens it in spring. Even so it is the accumulated influence of mutual understanding and common purpose that will effectively unite the British and the American peoples; not a formal alliance heralded round the globe as an accomplishment of diplomacy.

Those interested in seeing an approximation of the English-speaking peoples profess with good reason that their purpose is to promote the well-being of the whole world, by the preservation and diffusion of the common civilization which they hold as trustees for the humanity that is to be. The hope of a reign of peace on earth and good-will to men cannot fade from the heart of mankind. The prophets of Israel had a vision of the coming age; the Stoics dreamed of the whole world as an ordered city; Virgil sang his sweet song of humanity for a distressful time; and the Christian religion has kept alive the faith in the advent of the Kingdom of God. We also who speak the English tongue and feed our spirits on its literature, faint though we were after the late War from deferred hope, pluck up our courage as we contemplate the steady improvement in the relations between the British and the American peoples. If ever a new order is to be ushered in, the day will surely begin with the creation of sympathy between them. For the hastening of such a day Canada in her history, her character and her position holds a unique privilege, and, if she takes advantage of it, the world of the future will judge that she will have played a part given to few nations in the progress of humanity.

INDEX

For EU product safety concerns, contact us at Calle de José Abascal, 56–1°,
28003 Madrid, Spain or eugpsr@cambridge.org.

www.ingramcontent.com/pod-product-compliance
Ingram Content Group UK Ltd.
Pitfield, Milton Keynes, MK11 3LW, UK
UKHW020320140625
459647UK00018B/1939